Celebrating Animal Rescue

Stories that give hope
and renew our humanity.

Edited by Janet Vormittag
and Tricia L. McDonald

Celebrating Animal Rescue

ISBN 978-1-939294-37-1

Published by

CATS AND DOGS
A MAGAZINE DEVOTED TO COMPANION ANIMALS
www.catsanddogsmagazine.com

splatteredinkpress.com   catsanddogsmagazine.com

Dedication

To all the animals still waiting to be rescued.

Forward

If I had to choose one animal who was responsible for taking me down the one-way road of animal rescue, it would be Lucy, a black and white kitten my husband and I found at Mount Baldhead in Saugatuck, Michigan. We went to climb the sand dune to watch the sunset over Lake Michigan, but instead of a romantic evening, we found a partially paralyzed kitten covered with fleas. A trip to the vet revealed her back wasn't broken, but she didn't have control of her bowels or bladder. He recommended euthanasia, but I wanted to give her a chance.

Lucy never did regain use of her back legs, however she compensated with her front legs and shoulders and she was able to drag herself around. She could even pull herself up onto the couch. She was a happy cat and often snuck out the dog door to sit in the sun. She was the best mouser I've ever had by practicing patience—she let them come to her.

Lucy was prone to bladder infections and she hated the taste of antibiotics, but we muddled through, and I learned to squeeze her bladder to help with urination. Today if I found such a kitten I would take her for alternative treatment like acupuncture, but back in the 1980s I wasn't aware of any options. Today she would have also had a cart with wheels, even though mobility was never an issue with her.

Because of Lucy I became more in tune with animals and started volunteering. In 2006, I founded a local free publication, *Cats and Dogs, a Magazine Devoted to Companion Animals.* The monthly magazine focused on rescues, shelters and humane societies and promoted adoption and spay/neuter.

While organizing the magazine, I urged my friend Tricia L. McDonald to write a monthly column about her dog, Sally. Nine years later, she's still writing *Life with Sally* and has published three books about her quirky little white dog. Publishing those books led her to start her own publishing company, Splattered Ink Press.

Sally wasn't a rescue, but Tricia's second dog, Eli, was adopted from Wishbone Pet Rescue. The little guy had been at the Allegan County Animal Shelter until a Wishbone volunteer placed him in foster care.

Rescue is about people working together and giving each discarded animal a chance to find a new family. If everyone did what these people do—take in an animal in need, the problem would be solved.

After hearing the many stories of animal rescue, Tricia and I decided to put together this collection of stories. Some will make you laugh, while some will make you cry. You'll shake your head at some, and others will make you think. Our hope is that these stories will give hope and help renew humanity.

~ Janet Vormittag & Tricia L. McDonald

Table of Contents

Bulldog Christmas - *DeVonna R. Allison* 1

The One Eye Love - *Joelle Asmondy* 5

The More the Merrier, I Think - *Judith Marie Austin-Lieffers* .11

The Committee - *Jill Bannink-Albrecht* 17

Rescues' Rescue - *Linda Bengston* 23

Auntie Needs a New Cat - *Emily Bridson* 27

Amazing Grace - *Stacy Bullock* 31

Lena the Cat - *Wendy Merrick Burbank* 35

London, My Friend Forever - *Maylin Carretero* 39

My Little Rescue Friend - *Ada Chapman* 45

Taking Chances - *Andrea Collins* 49

Get Lost - *Linda Converse* 55

A Good Old Buddy - *Deb Cusic* 61

Big Boy - *Gina Devries* 65

Bud-Boo, W-underdog - *Lori Dishneau* 69

A Toast to Mr. Cranky Pants - *Patti Eddington* 75

A Dog Mystery - *Harold Garrecht* 81

How I Was Rescued - *Mary Aiello Gauntner* 85

Worm Crossing the Road - *Brian Gillie* 89

Waiting to Go Home - *Juley Harvey* 93

Getting Skunked - *Elizabeth F. Hill* 95

A Forever Home for Foxy - *Lenore Hirsch* 99

Found by Felines - Friendly and Feral - *Deanna Hotchkin* ..105

Changing My World - Jodi Jarvis-Therrian 109

A Catastrophic Miracle? - *Karen Anne Kazyak* 113

Side by Side - *Marty Kingsbury* 119

The Journey of Four Puppies - *Mary Kingsbury* 123

First Dogs - *Marty Kingsbury* 127

Seymour's Happenstance - *Karen Koger* 129

How Many Moms? - *Sharon Langeland* 135

The Fabulous Fin Finds Me - *Kendall Jameson* 141

A Country in Which You Once Lived - *Sarabeth Loomis* 145

A Chance Encounter - *Vonni Leaver* 151

Going Home - *Ali J. Shaw* 157

The Howler - *Eileen McVety* 163

A Day in Rescue I Will Never Forget - *Michele Melvin* 167

Miggy - *HJ Mayes* 171

Adding to the Number of Illegal Immigrants - ....

   Stephanie Medlock 177

The Ugliest Rat Dog - *Eleanor Whitney Nelson* 183

Growing into Grace - *Susan Newhof* 189

The French Feral - *Elizabeth Leis Newman* 195

The Cat with the Lemon-Lime Eyes - *Rochelle Newman* 201

Second Chance - *Karen Phelps* 207

How Stella... Once Fight Dog Bait...Got Her Groove Back -

   Marsha Porter 211

When Pinto Got Paroled - *Joan Potter* 217

The Perfect Cat with Many Imperfections - *Jane Urbanski* ..223

They Bread Him That Way - *Rachel Wolf* 231

Take Me Home! - *Kate O'Neill* 237

Adoption - *D.G. Messinger* 243

Love is Love's Gift - *Aaron Hamm* 249

A Two Way Street - *Sally Karasiewicz* 255

Slum Buddy - *Daniel R. Tardona* 259

From Death Row to a Forever Home - *Gayle Thompson* 265

You Just Never Know - *Michele J. Dunckel* 269

Turtle Rescue - *Sue Merrell* 275

About the Editors 279

Bulldog Christmas

By DeVonna R. Allison

It was the week before Christmas and my husband and I had just arrived home from the movies when a car pulled into our driveway. Out in the country we don't get many unannounced visitors, but squinting through the headlights I recognized our daughter's car and went out to greet her and her boyfriend. I was not prepared for what would leap from the car as she opened the door. There was a blur of white, and the unmistakable form of an English bulldog wriggled around my knees.

"What in the world?" I stammered.

"Mom, she's so cute and she's lost and I think she's sick and ..." our daughter rushed through her words. I could tell she was trying to convince Dad and me to keep the dog before the question was even asked. I was enamored by the dog's friendly demeanor, but when I reached down to pet her I felt rough patches of scaling flesh and sparse fur. Obviously uncomfortable, the dog shook her head violently and nonetheless gave me a wide bully grin in response to my attentions.

"Be careful, don't touch it, that dog's sick," my husband warned, frowning. I knew what he was thinking; he didn't want to infect our own elderly dog with whatever it was this stranger carried. And he was thinking we didn't need another dog, and I knew why.

In the spring of the year we'd lost our beloved 10-year-old American pitbull terrier to cancer and it had broken our

hearts, especially Earl's. He and Ebony Rose had been inseparable. Wherever Earl was, that's where you'd find Ebony,
whether it was out in the garage while he worked on his
various projects or outside the bathroom door while Earl
showered. She was Daddy's baby, no doubt about it, and the
day we put her down, Earl's grief was palpable.

We still had our son's childhood pet, a pound rescue we'd
had for 12 years and now here we were faced with another
obviously sick dog. Earl seemed determined to guard his heart
against getting attached to the bulldog.

Our daughter explained how she found the dog wandering
the streets in town and how the dog approached various
strangers in a parking lot, trying to enter their cars. It was a
typical Michigan December evening, cold and blowing and
hinting at snow. Our daughter's heart broke over the dog's
plight so she and her boyfriend allowed it to climb into her
car. They'd brought the bulldog straight to us.

Begging us to keep the dog overnight until they could figure out what to do with her (they already had two dogs of their
own) we agreed, Earl quite reluctantly, to allow the dog to
sleep in our garage for the night. Under the overhead lights of
the garage the full extent of the dog's pitiful condition became
apparent. She had drainage coming from one ear, her eyes
were rheumy, and in addition to what we suspected was a
case of mange, she was absolutely covered in fleas. When
offered food and water she ignored the food, but drank two
bowls full of water. It was shocking and a bit sickening to see
the dog's terrible condition, but what struck me most was her
upbeat attitude and natural friendliness.

Earl was quiet, so it was hard to guess his thoughts as we
closed the dog in the garage for the night. I trusted his love of
animals would lead him to help us care for this poor dog.

The next morning he was the first one out in the garage. He was pleased when he found she hadn't had an accident in the garage or gotten into anything. I smiled as I watched him interact with the bulldog out in the yard, and my faith in his love of animals was rewarded when he came inside and announced, "We've got to get that dog to the vet."

As we headed to the veterinarian's office, Earl cradled the bulldog's large head between his knees and could watch her flesh literally crawling with fleas. "I can't understand how someone could let such a beautiful dog get in such terrible condition," he said as he murmured comforting words to the dog to calm her.

At the vet's office the doctor informed us that the dog was indeed an English bulldog mix, about 2-years-old. He also confirmed our suspicions; she had mange. What we'd been unable to see was a horrific double ear infection. We told the doctor how we came to have her in our possession and he asked us what we were going to call her. I was about to state we weren't keeping her, when Earl piped in, "Her name is Molly." I looked at my husband in surprise and mirth; he had succumbed to Molly's bulldog charms.

Thus began the treatment of her ills. The vet cleaned her painful ears deeply and she stood and took it stoically. He gave us drops to put in her ears several times a day, ran a thread of Frontline down her back to kill the fleas and scheduled her for mange dip treatments over the course of the next few months. In the meantime, we bought her an extra-large dog crate to comfortably house her 60-pound frame, as she had to live in the garage until her mange was under control.

We did eventually find Molly's original family. When we asked to be reimbursed for the expenses we incurred from getting her healthy again, they told us we could keep her instead, and so we have.

Today Molly is the picture of good-natured bulldog health and is a happy obedient member of our family. She is my husband's constant companion, following him around the house or yard as he works outside. She has the run of our many acres and her affection is as boundless as her enthusiasm for play. It's as if she knows we saved her.

DeVonna R. Allison is a freelance writer whose work has been featured in various print and online publications. Her work has been included in several anthologies including Proud to Be, Volume III, published by Southeast Missouri University Press and Chicken Soup for the Soul; Miracles Happen. She's won contests for her writing from Southern California Genealogical Society and the University of Maine at Machias. She and her husband Earl are Marine Corps veterans and enjoy live music performances and travel. They make their home in Southern Michigan where they live with their three rescued dogs and one rescued cat.

The One Eye Love

Honorable Mention

By Joelle Asmondy

When I first met Gabby, her eye socket was swollen, giving the false impression that her right eye still lived there. If you looked closer, you could see the stitches closing it. Permanently.

Standing in front of her kennel, I watched her sleeping. I could see her crooked underbite, see her ears folded inside out like an umbrella on a windy day, and hear her never-to-be-mistaken-for-a-dainty-princess snore.

She was perfect.

The details were few. Blossom, as she was known then, was a 10-month-old puggle who had been attacked by a dog, resulting in several tooth-sized divots on her face that you can see when the light hits her just right—and a terminal lack of peripheral vision. Her first family was going to have her put down, but her vet (also a pet rescue facility) knew she was adoptable if the family would consider relinquishing her. They did, and that's how I came to meet Gabby that day.

I work at a school that trains pet groomers. We provide free services to rescued pets to help them put their best paw forward on adoption day. That afternoon, I had been working in my office when our Lead Instructor told me about a cute dog I just had to see. That was it. I was done. I made a quick phone call to make sure I wasn't walking home and into a divorce, opened the crate, and picked Gabby up for the first time.

I've never seen a puggle like her—I mean, aside from the eye thing. She's got a muzzle like a boxer, a tail like a pug that curls when she gets excited, and the body the shape and color of a beagle. She bays like a beagle and snores like a pug— sometimes when she's looking right at you. On that first meeting she smelled clean and fresh from her bath as I tucked her under my chin. She sighed deeply and went back to sleep, snoring loudly.

I tried not to love her. I really did. Resistance, as they say, was futile. I already had three cats, but they fell in love with her, too. My partner established a list of rules for a new dog-enhanced household, and promptly threw them away. I thought there would be some trait that would appear during her sleep-over that would mean she was meant for someone else, but...nothing. I completed the adoption process and she came home for keeps.

She went through a lot of change in a short period of time. The attack. The surgery. Her first groom. Adoption into a new family and surroundings. Her first snow. That first weekend she also "became a woman," as my mother would say, and went back to the vet for a little fixing up.

A new name. Blossom didn't seem to fit her. She didn't really respond to it. What else do you do when you have a one-eyed dog, but look up names of famous female pirates? Gabrielle was too formal. When we said, *Gabby* for the first time, she turned immediately to us and walked over as if to ask what had taken us so long.

The first few days we learned a lot about caring for a dog sans an eye. We quickly realized that we needed those bumper things on our coffee table that you use for babies. Gabby swiftly forgot she had nothing to check her passenger side with and would run into things—furniture, the walls, me. She figured it out so fast that we forgot she was compensating. We came to the conclusion that dogs with two eyes were just bragging. Life just went on.

When you work at a grooming school, you have the privilege of bringing your dog to work with you every day. Gabby loves our team, who dote on her with endless love and attention. As you might imagine, she gets a few curious stares. The kids are my favorite. Often, the younger ones just look as though they know something is missing, but can't quite put a finger on what it is. It's a good teaching moment about diversity and adversity. The adults are more entertaining. When asked what's wrong with her eye, I usually respond with, "Nothing, why?" and watch as they either stammer and/or freak out trying to tell me that something is seriously wrong with my dog. Sometimes I enjoy a puzzled stare as they wonder whether I must be crazy not to have noticed she's shy a blinker on the right side. More often than not, I pull out a few one-liners to explain things:

"She lost it in a card game."

"That was extra, so we got the basic package."

"It's at the cleaners."

Or my favorite: "Hold on everybody—it's missing again!" I can be kind of a jerk that way.

I went from smitten to head-over-heels with Gabby in seconds. I've grown up with cats and dogs all my life, but there is something special about her. We "get" each other on a level that borders on the ridiculous. We sigh at the same time while

7

watching movies. I'm told that when we're sleeping, it's tough to decide who is snoring loudest. My teeth would still look like hers if not for the braces I wore as a kid, and I can't see two feet without my glasses. Upon meeting Gabby for the first time, my employer remarked, "She suits you." I'm still working out what that means.

Many rescue stories are filled with tales about how the dog pulled someone from a burning building or provided comfort to someone waging a battle with cancer. Ours is much simpler, though no less meaningful. Gabby didn't cure me of disease or rescue me from a fiery death, but she saved me just the same. She filled a hole in my life and heart I didn't know I had. She makes people smile wherever she goes.

I can sum it up with this last story. It's a post from my Facebook page back in April 2014 when my partner and I had nothing on our minds but a dozen errands to run:

"My heart must have changed since we welcomed this pirate pup into our lives. We had a long list of things to do on this beautiful Saturday, but one look back at the house as we backed out of the driveway and saw that face looking out the window. All plans have been scrapped. We are now taking a drive with no real destination. Just the three of us, enjoying the day."

The title was inspired by Gabby and a great song by Heywood Banks, entitled "One Eye Love." If you need a laugh, it's definitely worth a listen!

Joelle Asmondy *earned her B.A. in Art from Western Michigan University and has been an active artist, producing fine art as well as graphic design, for the last 20 years. She parlayed* *these experiences into a successful career in editing, sales, marketing, and design.*

Joelle shares her home with her partner of 19 years, their two cats, and Gabby, the Wonder Puggle. She is an avid reader who also enjoys working in her garden. When she's not working or writing, you can usually find her in her art studio or the local bookstore.

The More the Merrier, I Think

By Judith Marie Austin-Lieffers

Hearing a truck door slam, I stepped outside into the mid-October sun on our side porch and forced a smile for my least favorite neighbor.

"Hey, Judy," Cathy called from the middle of the driveway, waving a hefty arm. "We stopped by to return the miter saw Bob borrowed last week."

"Great," I said, pushing my phony smile wider. "Ross isn't here, but you can leave it anywhere in the barn workshop."

Cathy gestured to the open barn door. "That's what Bob's doing." She walked toward the house. "Did you know you've got at least three wild cats in your barn?"

I kept the smile pasted on my face. "Actually there are four, but the little black one is shy. He's probably hiding." I had to work to keep my tone light.

Born and raised on a beef cattle farm, Cathy eagerly shared with anybody and everybody her loudly-voiced opinion that any animal that couldn't be butchered or milked wasn't worth the money to feed it.

Joining me on the porch, she said, "You know cats carry diseases."

"All of our cats, dogs and horses have been vaccinated and spayed or neutered," I told her for possibly the hundred and fifty-seventh time since I'd married Ross ten years ago and moved from suburban Chicago to rural western Michigan.

In my prior life, single and renting a two-bedroom coach house in Chicago, I'd still managed to adopt three "alley" cats and rescue an English setter. When Ross, a college friend, lost his wife, we'd re-connected and, within six months, were married. Since he lived in Michigan, I moved all three cats and the setter with me.

Living on 40 acres of Michigan farmland was hugely different from Chicago, but I loved it. We had four horses, a big horse barn, a little hay barn, eight acres of pasture, 30 acres for growing hay, and a three-bedroom, three-bath home. Plenty of room for the horses, three rescued dogs, an ever-changing number of cats, and us.

"Just how many cats do you have now?" Cathy asked, her increasing distaste for anything feline obvious on her round face.

I did a quick head count. "Pretty sure we're at about eighteen."

Cathy gasped. "How in the name of God did you get eighteen cats?"

I sighed audibly. "Well, Cathy, we had seventeen, and one more showed up three days ago. Ross named him Scruffy."

"They're not all in the house, are they?" she demanded.

I gestured toward the barn workshop. "No, I told you, I'm pretty sure we have four in the barn workshop, two in the barn feed room, three on the back porch, and three in the garage."

I could see the wheels spinning in her head. "That means you have six cats in your house?" Clearly aghast, Cathy stared at me as though I'd lost my mind.

I stuffed my hands into my jeans pockets and rocked back on my heels. "Yep."

She looked horrified. "And Ross puts up with this?"

"Ross thinks over half the cats belong to him," I said. "Gandalf, Toes, Mikey, Snickers and Oreo, Charley, Tuxedo Man, BC, BW, Cohort and...," I thought quickly. "Oh, and Scruffy. Ross insisted we keep him because he purrs so loudly and just burrows into your..."

"Ross doesn't even like cats," Cathy interrupted.

"Well, maybe he didn't until we married and I moved three cats from Chicago with me. But he sure loves cats now."

Cathy gazed at me as though I was a very young child who just didn't get it. "Judy, you don't have to feed them. Just because people from the city drive out here and drop them off, it doesn't mean you have to take them in."

A gust of wind blew my curly hair into my eyes, and I brushed it away impatiently. "When Ross and I accepted the responsibility of taking care of these cats, it was a commitment that includes feeding them. And as long as we have cat food outside, any stray cat wandering by is going to help himself. That's just the way it is," I said. "It's not like we planned to have eighteen cats. The drop-offs just show up here. And I can't tell a feral cat where to have her kittens." I shrugged, trying to lighten up. "They don't speak English."

I didn't tell her about the pet bed heating pads in all the cat houses Ross had built. No point in her trying to have both of us committed.

Cathy pursed her lips, still staring at me as though I'd grown two heads.

"The biggest problem is the dairy farm across the road," I explained. "Dave's got enough issues single-handedly running a dairy farm of 70-plus head of cattle. He wants as many cats as possible to control the mice population so he won't consider spaying or neutering. But he doesn't have the time to deal with a dozen feral cats. He doesn't feed them, he doesn't provide water so when the females get pregnant, they come to our farm to have their kittens because this is where they find food and water. Cats aren't stupid."

If Bob hadn't interrupted us by calling out to tell Cathy it was time to go, I'm sure she would have told me who the stupid one was. Luckily, she left, taking her tight lips and condemning eyes back up the road to their old farmhouse. No animals there.

I blew out a huge sigh and shook my head, the curls flying again. It was a good thing Ross wasn't home. He didn't like Cathy either.

I looked skyward and thanked God that Cathy hadn't walked out to the hay barn. She would have heard the kittens for sure.

Two weeks ago, Ross found five tiny kittens snuggled in the hay bales. Over the next few days we discovered they belonged to a feral female from the dairy farm. We called her Cranky Mama Kitty. Not at all tame or friendly, she hissed and growled anytime we came near. But she'd had a litter earlier in the year and took good care of them, leading them back across the road to the dairy farm when they were old enough.

But something was wrong. When I'd gone out to the barn early this morning to get hay for the horses, all five kittens were screaming and crying for their mother. Cranky Mama Kitty was nowhere to be found. I'd been keeping an eye on the barn out the kitchen window, trying to see if she'd returned, but I hadn't seen her all day.

It was late afternoon now, and I could still hear them crying. Opening the door, I carefully checked the protective hay bale pocket Ross and I had made to keep them safe and warm, and they were all wriggling and screaming. No Cranky Mama Kitty. I couldn't believe she'd abandoned them. Something dire must have happened.

Heading back to the garage, I grabbed a pet carrier. Bundling them all in, I took them into the mudroom where I pulled out a large, tall, clear plastic bin, put in a pet bed heating pad wrapped in a towel to keep them warm, added a large dog bowl filled with cat litter, carefully put all five kittens, four brown tabbies and a tuxedo black and white, on the heating pad and made a run to Petco for cat milk replacement.

They couldn't be more than two weeks old. Hardly bigger than a good-sized mouse.

Home again, I Googled, "How to Bottle Feed Kittens" and found all the info I needed.

 We got through a couple weeks of bottle feeding, weaning them into kitten food and kept them until Thanksgiving weekend when my niece came up from Chicago with her fiancé. They'd lost two of their cats in the last few months, one to cancer and one to kidney failure, and we were hoping they might take at least one of the kittens.

They took two; the black and white female they named Mimi and a sweet brown tabby male they named Moosie. Both cat-lovers, they wanted very affectionate cats that would sleep with them and cuddle on the sofa with them, and that's exactly what they got. Lindsey's Faccbook page is filled with Mimi and Moosie photos.

The other three kittens, two brown marble tabbies and a brown standard tabby, we took to Faithful to Felines, a local non-profit organization that takes socialized kittens and cats, gives them all their vaccines, checks for fleas, worms, and ear mites, and spays or neuters, all free, then places them in local Petco pet stores to be adopted for a nominal charge.

We were told all three were adopted the first day because they were so outgoing, sweet and friendly.

I'm just glad Cathy never found out. I really didn't want to hear what she would have said about 23 cats!

Judith Marie Austin-Lieffers has always loved animals. Well, everything with fur anyway. That's why, when she finally married at 50-somtehing, it was to a guy with horses, dogs and a cat. She immediately added three more cats, another dog and another horse.

Fortunately, she is a freelance writer and sets her own hours which gives her unlimited time for the current animal population explosion in seriously rural Michigan. Irresponsible people who drop off unwanted animals and the neighboring dairy farmer who refuses to spay or neuter his feral cats keep her whisker-deep in furry love.

The Committee

By Jill Bannink-Albrecht

I was on a euthanasia committee. Almost on a daily basis, I walked into the cat room at my local shelter and selected cats for euthanasia due to lack of space. As an open admission shelter, we had to take in every cat and dog that came through the door and limited kennel space left us scrambling to find places for everyone. Like a cruel game of musical chairs, we often had more cats than cages, and as a result, I was left picking cats as candidates for euthanasia.

I will admit that after months of this process, I became hardened and blocked off a section of my mind from thinking too deeply about my actions. I played a mental game with myself by finding justification for selecting certain cats. A visibly ill cat, suffering from upper respiratory infection, a common shelter illness, made an easy target for my selection process. After all, the animal was ill. I could also justify selecting an unadoptable cat. In the shelter world, animals are often judged on their adoptability—how likely someone from the public would adopt the animal and therefore, free up kennel space for another animal. An unadoptable animal just clogged up precious, limited space. In the world of felines, urinary issues, behavioral issues, plain colors such as black or black/brown tiger, and old age all contributed to a cat being unadoptable.

When I first began working at the shelter, I was astonished to learn that the general consensus was that even 5-year-old animals were viewed as too old and often passed over for younger dogs and cats. Dealing with the death of a pet is a traumatic process, and I think people, even at a subconscious level, see an older animal and begin imagining that reality on the horizon instead of several years away. Plus, an adult animal simply can't compete with the initial appeal of cuddly, playful kittens and tiny puppies, complete with baby fat rolls. Yet, older animals make excellent pets because they are so grateful to have another chance at life, and they show that gratitude on a daily basis. My shelter mission became promoting adoption for those animals five years and older, because everyone deserves to be loved in their golden years of life.

One day, the shelter took in a large orange and white tiger cat named Tyson. He lived his whole life with his one owner, who decided that due to business obligations he no longer had time for Tyson in his life. Tyson was 5-years-old and four-paw declawed. Declawed cats are coveted by many people and often get adopted quickly. Much to my surprise and despite my best efforts (which sometimes involved me literally dropping him into potential adopters laps), he didn't get adopted. One woman stroked his back lovingly and told me what a wonderful, friendly cat he was but he was simply too old. As the months passed, other members of the euthanasia committee suggested him as a choice on three separate occasions. My protests to this plan bought him more time, at least temporarily. Every day, I looked up from my desk at the shelter to see him in his kennel, his orange and white front legs dangling through the bars as he tried to get comfortable.

In agony over his fate, I finally decided to take him home, and he blossomed into a wonderful cat with a playful personality. He loved to sit on my lap facing me so he could look right into my eyes. He enjoyed playing tricks on my cranky old Chihuahua, Oliver. Sometimes, he hid behind the corner of the wall and would jump out at Oliver as he passed by, eliciting a grumble from my dog. Tyson enjoyed playing and at night he would jump at the light switch, trying to turn on the light so I would join him in a game with his favorite catnip toy. Occasionally, he dived right on my chest while I was sleeping, startling me in his attempt to get attention. I enjoyed his companionship and love, but sadly, just a year after I rescued him, he developed a rare form of cancer. Despite a surgery performed by the best specialists in the state, he could not be saved. His death traumatized me, and I felt like we both got cheated out of many good years we could have spent together. At the time, I didn't realize that his life and his rescue story touched me in a deeper, more profound way.

After several years at the shelter, I became burned out by my job. My position on the euthanasia committee, combined with compassion fatigue, really began to take a toll on my mind and body. I disagreed with the way shelter politics became more important than caring for the animals, and I developed an intense bitterness that colored the way I viewed everything in my world. I felt like a husk of my former self, full of inner turmoil, anxiety, depression, and anger.

I left the shelter and the animal welfare world and took a job at an office. Months went by and I listlessly went through the motions of daily life. I made an effort to appear normal and content to everyone in my life, but I felt a deep unhappiness and a lack of purpose. Animal welfare is my passion and my true calling in life. Even as a child, I sensed this destiny though I couldn't verbalize the idea. At the age of nine, I drew up flyers urging people to save the rainforest jaguars and hung them on telephone poles around my neighborhood, disappointed that I couldn't start a movement. Clearly, I needed more meaning in my life than my office job, and I began thinking of entering the animal welfare field again. This time, I wanted to make sure I had control over what happened to the animals in my care by establishing my own animal rescue.

This May, I established Tyson's Place Animal Rescue. Thinking of Tyson, who faced euthanasia several times due to his age, I realized there needed to be a rescue that focused on saving adult animals from life and, ultimately, untimely death in a shelter. Reflecting more on my experiences, I thought about the times the shelter took in older animals whose owners had passed away. These animals were often traumatized by the loss of their owners and then thrust into the noisy, crowded, frightening world of a shelter, where they were unlikely to be adopted due to their advanced age. My rescue will focus on helping terminally ill people take care of their animals so they can experience the joy of that bond until their last days. Everyone, pets and people alike, deserve the opportunity to be loved in their last years or days left. Plus, the rescue will be able to take in these pets after the owners pass away, allowing these animals to bypass the shelter world.

Though Tyson only graced my life briefly, he left with me a lasting impression on the harsh reality of shelter life for older animals. I may have rescued him by taking him home, but he rescued me in a more meaningful way, guiding me back to my true purpose in life and allowing me to remember what I rescued him from so I can help other animals avoid facing a euthanasia committee. I am truly celebrating my rescue by turning that word rescue in an active, empowered word that will branch out into many new adoption success stories, honoring Tyson along the way.

Jill Bannink-Albrecht *is founder and president of Tyson's Place Animal Rescue, which is dedicated to assisting terminally ill people with caring for and finding new families for their pets (www.tysonsplacerescue.org). Jill and her husband Michael live in a haunted old farmhouse in Byron Center, Michigan, complete with a variety of cats and dogs. She has degrees in journalism and history from Grand Valley State University. A lifelong animal advocate, she is especially passionate about senior rescue animals. She can be reached at tysonsplacerescue@gmail.com.*

Rescues' Rescue

By Linda Bengston

A soft "mewp" followed by the thump of a cat landing on my desk jar me from my thoughts. Daisy moves to my lap and pats my face with a soft paw. She touches tears, and then nestles her silky face into my neck.

Daisy, as I will learn, is part of a finely choreographed campaign to comfort me.

I have agreed to write a letter. My client's employee has days to live, and my client doesn't want his clients to learn of the death through the newspaper. Rather, he wants me to write a personal letter that can be mailed immediately. I am best suited to write the letter, my client says, because I have worked with the man, I understand him beyond his professional self, I know his love for his family and career, I understand how much he values the company that values him.

Of course, I accept. Who better than I to capture the essence of this determined, talented professional with whom I've worked, played, and known as father, husband, coach, co-worker, dreamer? I feel honored to accept this sacred task.

The space between the accepting and the doing, I soon learn, is cavernous. Remembering a dynamic, living, breathing person and writing about that person in the past tense breaks my heart. Tears stream down my face as I fill the computer screen with words. Chest-heaving sobs stop the flow. I am attempting to capture the essence of a person. How could I have been so naïve as to think I could easily do this? I have agreed to encapsulate a human life that is ending decades before its allotted three score and ten.

Well into the task, absorbed in misery, I begin to notice a pattern. Maizie comes quietly into my office, pats my leg, and meows to be picked up. Our first rescue, Maizie is our Earth Mother. A tortie, Maizie was taken from the streets along with her litter two years ago. Soon after weaning her litter, she adopted the kittens of a mother who couldn't nurse. The first few days Maizie lived with us, we would hear her melancholy cries throughout the house. Soon, however, examining us from deep-set eyes beneath long lashes, she apparently decided my husband and I would be her next litter. Decision made, she immediately claimed a spot on our king-size bed and in our hearts. If Maizie wore shoes, they would be Birkenstocks.

I pick Maizie up distractedly. She pats my face and burrows into my lap, broadcasting a loud, comforting purr. Some 40 minutes later, Maizie springs gently down and walks quietly from my office. Soon, another visitor arrives.

Also a rescue, Lizzie is our sleek, gray Russian princess. We envision her comfortable in tiara and ropes of pearls; she has never forgotten that ancient Egyptians worshipped cats. Despite her generally royal demeanor, Lizzie bounds onto my desk and then to my lap, patting my face with tiny paws that smear tears. Like Maizie, she nestles and begins to purr, wrapping her paws around my arm. Because Lizzie so obviously prefers my husband's company to mine, I feel the tiniest bit honored that she has chosen to spend time with me.

Lizzie's nap ends much like Maizie's—she wakes, stretches, pats my face, and pads quietly out. I return to my sorrowful task.

In minutes, I hear a quiet meow and see Emily rubbing her cheek against the door frame. Our contrary, solitary calico, Emily is stand-offish and none too fond of petting, stroking, or snuggling. We've commented that we should have named her Garbo. Another rescue, Emily never seems quite comfortable anywhere in our house with her sisters or with us. She always appears a bit distracted, and we joke that her long whiskers are likely picking up some cat station in a far distant land. She pats my leg, looks up, and meows.

"Hello, Sweetie. What's up?" I ask, reaching to pet her.

To my surprise, she leaps onto my desk, puts her face close to mine, and meows. Then Emily pats my face, nuzzles my neck, and curls into my lap. Surprised, I stroke her and return to typing. She stays, purring and snuggling for some 30 minutes.

Emily is gone only a short time when Daisy arrives. A silky champagne tabby, Daisy is our Goldie Hawn cat. Funny, frisky, and playful, she would be the one to accessorize with rhinestone-embellished, heart-shaped sunglasses. She absolutely knows the entire world adores her. Daisy follows what has become a familiar script.

Throughout the day, from my first explosive sob to my last sighing sniffle, I am the object of a carefully choreographed campaign of comfort apparently hatched by four cats in some quiet corner of our house. One by one, they share their soft paws, vibrating purrs, and comforting presence. Dark eyes hold mine, silky heads stretch for nose-to-nose kisses, whiskers tickle my cheeks. Our four furry daughters offer wordless understanding and consolation. If they could share my tears, I'm certain they would.

Hours later, I have portrayed a life not perfectly but well. Maizie's gentle meow at my door is the period to my gut-wrenching day.

Relaxed, glass of wine in hand, I am recounting my day to my husband when I stop mid-sentence. Until this moment, I have considered rescuing something we have done for our cats. Now I know differently. Maizie, Lizzie, Emily, and Daisy are as much rescuers as rescues. Sensing my distress, they did all they could to relieve it. Their wordless, eloquent comfort eased my soul-deep sadness.

Today, our rescues rescued me.

Linda Bengston shares her home, her life, her heart, and her bed with five purebred-by-heart, four-legged, furry, rescued daughters: Maizie, Lizzie, Daisy, Emily, and Iris. Oh, and with her husband Doug Chestnut.

Linda spent her career writing, editing, and marketing for business. Over 40+ years, she worked for several national corporations and spent the last decade of her career doing freelance work. She still does freelance and pro bono projects and is experimenting with writing memories. Rescues' Rescue is her first memory to be published.

Auntie Needs a New Cat

By Emily Bridson

I had always grown up with cats as a child and loved spending days in the country looking after wandering cats and their fluffy kittens. When I became an adult, moving from apartment to apartment, I put the thought out of my head of opening my home to a pet.

As I entered my late 30s, I saw the joy other friends and families had with their pets and I started doing my research. I asked others what they loved about their cats, what breeds they liked and why, how they came to find their furriest family members—and my own hunt began.

One of my friends spoke highly of Russian blues—their exotic looks, intelligence, and athleticism. I Googled the breed and came to love them. I started looking up local shelters to see if any had such a cat, and sure enough, there was one available. The first time I met Bella; she plopped on her side and was eager to have me pet her fur. She was a loving and sweet girl. I brought her home that day.

I took advantage of the free physical that came with her adoption a couple of months later and that is where things start to go wrong. As the vet looked in her ear all I heard was, "Hmmm." She couldn't get a clear view down her ear canal. After some very expensive tests, it was determined that my beautiful girl had an inoperable ear tumor. The vet explained to me that cats have a high tolerance to pain, so when she starts showing symptoms, it was probably significant to her.

I had Bella for six months in all and she was the happiest, craziest cat I ever knew. I felt very fortunate for the time we spent together. It was love at first sight and a devastating hole in my heart to see her go. The day I had to drive her to the vet to be put to sleep was one of the worst times ever. I still get teary-eyed when I think about it.

A couple of weeks later, my pet-loving family had big plans for me. My sister immediately hatched an idea to hand over one of her two cats to me. You see, my brother-in-law took in an unexpected cat from a friend and now they were over their limit. They had a smaller house and a dog. My 6-year-old niece, Fiona, quickly saw that her cat was the one being offered up. The wheels in her head started turning and she became a girl on a mission—to find me a cat so hers could stay at their house.

Fiona was decidedly pragmatic about my loss and the quick recovery that was in my future. She declared it was time for me to get a new cat. I explained to her why I wasn't ready, and silly me, I told her we could look a little. We hopped back on the website from Bella's rescue center and started looking at all the possibilities—big cats, fat cats, extra furry ones, little cute kittens (I have a feeling you know the drill). We giggled, laughed and worked our way methodically down page after page. In the end, a short list was compiled of cats to keep in mind.

Fiona, being the smart girl that she is, saw that these cats would be at the local PetCo that afternoon and we should go have a look. I called up the rescue group, and sure enough, they could arrange for the cats to be there. I told her we were just going to look; no cats were coming home with us. I was excited, though, to see their personalities come to life.

To my dismay, the cat I was really interested was sick, so she did not make the trip. Our second choice, though, was ready to greet us. She was a long, lanky calico with a tail like a monkey. This kitty had pretty green eyes, a very friendly disposition, and her meow was distinct and loud. My niece promptly declared she was the one and that we had found my new cat to take home!

We reviewed the ground rules of "just coming to look" but she promptly walked me through all the reasons why I needed a new cat and why this one met my requirements. I had to agree with her. She did a great job of presenting a solid argument. We had to buy her a transport cage and all the items a cat needed, as I was royally unprepared for my new family member.

That was the best decision I made, under the influence of Fiona. The first order of business on the way home was a new name. I had a beautiful name chosen for her, which was promptly discarded by Fiona. We kept throwing names around all the while MEOW! MEOW! MEOW! was all that could be heard from our new guest. That's it, we thought—why not name her Meow Meow? My niece giggled and that sealed the deal.

Now my sister, on the other hand, was mad when we told her what we had done that day. She thought a nice cat from her house would be packing its bags shortly and be sent off to live with me. I think my brother-in-law quickly saw through my niece's scheme and helped my sister come to understand I had been bamboozled a little that day.

This was three years ago and Meow Meow has been a blessing every day. I treasure her when I am greeted at the door or breathed on in the morning to prepare her breakfast. Her favorite game is when I chase her around the house. I couldn't be happier to know I was able to provide a safe, loving home for her. My only wish now is to bring a second cat into our lives and I can't wait for that to happen.

Emily Bridson is an Engagement Manager for CQL, a Grand Rapids, Michigan based digital agency. With a passion for local government, she currently sits on the planning commission and parks and recreation commission for the city of Kentwood, Michigan. She earned her bachelor's degree in Liberal Arts from the University of Central Florida, her master's degree in Athletic Administration from Michigan State University, and recently earned her MBA from Northwood University. Emily is active in TEDxGandRapids as well as the Humane Society of West Michigan (www.hswestmi.org).

Amazing Grace

By Stacy Bullock

"She is kind of cute," my Mom said as I showed her the picture in the ad on the Craigslist posting. The buff colored Lhasa Apso /poodle mix with the curly tail and slight underbite had caught her eye. A glimmer of hope came into my heart. We had just lost our lovable yorkie, Oz. It was with heavy, empty hearts that we had just started considering loving another. Since I was three years old, I had always had a dog by my side and in my life and felt really lost without one. It seemed every dog I called on at rescues, shelters, or breeders had just been adopted or sold. We wanted to get an older dog rather than a puppy because it would already be trained and easier for our lifestyle. Besides it seemed like they knew and were always grateful for getting the "good life" they so deserved.

Her name was Gracie Lou and her family got her from a relative—she had been in three homes before they got her. They were a loving, responsible family and wanted the best for her. They wanted to find her a forever home because they could not give her the time she deserved with their busy lifestyle. They came up with an adoption process and had an application online. They reviewed all applicants and as a family chose the one they felt would be the best fit for her. We were so excited and blessed to be chosen as her new family and felt it was meant to be. As soon as we met her we fell in love with this little girl. She was just so very sweet in temperament and just the right combination of fun, playful, and happy as well as calm and content to make the perfect addition to our family.

Gracie fit right in from the start. Our cat, Merry (adopted from Harbor Humane Society), and she became instant friends from the moment we brought her in the door. They are cute together and we can tell they enjoy each other's company. My parents are retired and Gracie became Mom's shadow. If she is not by her side, she is in her lap. My parents are home with her all the time so she gets a lot of love and attention. She is spoiled and well loved by us all.

Our family has been through some rough patches lately. That is why I started saying Gracie is "My Amazing Grace." She has helped get us through all the challenges we have had to face. It is always nice to have a furry friend by your side when difficult times happen in life. They never judge and give such unconditional love and support—that is the best therapy in the world in my opinion. For me, I seem to be falling into a state of depression. Life was not going the way I had planned, as it rarely ever seems to for anyone. I had found out about some medical conditions and learning what I had known in my heart for years, that I could never be a mom, still devastated me. Then losing my little Ozzie bear, I was just so heartbroken. Gracie gave my life meaning and purpose again. She brought my smile back. It is such a joy that she loves to dress up and be "girly." Mom and I always have fun shopping for her. She loves to play and her silly side always makes me laugh. She will grab a toy and rub and roll on it, then set it down and run through the house as if on a racetrack. She is also a motivator. She gets us out walking and helps encourage a healthier lifestyle that we always seem to struggle with.

At the end of April of this year my dad had a sudden, massive, almost fatal, heart attack. It was scary and stressful, and it helped to have Gracie to cuddle when I was afraid and upset. When Dad came home from the hospital, Gracie never left his side as he started on the road to recovery. He had a defibrillator and pacemaker put in, as well as stents. It was a miracle he made it. Less than 10% do who have this type of heart attack called "sudden death." Our family is feeling very blessed and one of the many miracles was Gracie coming into our lives at a time when we needed her most. With her carefree, happy nature and always wagging, bushy tail she has warmed our hearts and her unconditional love helps us to grow stronger.

There is a saying; *Dogs are not our whole lives but make our lives whole.* I truly believe this because my Amazing Grace sure has and now it is difficult to tell who has rescued who!

Stacy Bullock is from Comstock Park where she lives with her parents, Les and Sharon Bullock. She has two girls--Merry (14), a kitty adopted from Harbor Humane Society, and Gracie (6) a Lhasa poodle mix. Stacy works at Pet Supplies Plus on Alpine and has been there since it opened in 1993. She really enjoys helping customers with their pet care needs. She has had a lot of training, including certification as a pet nutrition advisor. Stacy has always been an animal lover and advocate of responsible pet ownership, as well as adoption.

Lena the Cat

Honorable Mention

By Wendy Merrick Burbank

If Lena the Cat still lived here
she would curl into that bowl
of paperclips on the worktable
the way she wound herself

into every container. Veritably,
she couldn't pad by a vessel
without trying it out, furling
and unfurling incrementally

to fill its bounds. Lena was rescued
for the first time, in utero,
on the spring night her mother
showed up pregnant --

sleek but for the swell
of babies, part-Siamese,
regal and importunately social.
We named her Isis

after the goddess of children.
When she demanded to give birth
in my lap, I placed her in a blanketed
basket and kept my hands

where she wanted,
on her rump and rippling pelvis,
until she was done. One awful day
one year later, Isis's daughter Lena

coiled into a slop bucket
with an inch of heating oil
left in it after a furnace cleaning,
wicking the poison with her soft grey self.

When she sensed something
of what she had done she began to rid
herself of the viscous toxin
the only way she knew how. Later on,

she got more baths than we count
and through it all she railed heroically
against being saved, leaving her rescuers
clawed and bleeding.

The vet said there's nothing
to be done but the bathing.
She'll live or she'll die.
Her fate depends on which organs
the oil attacks. Relying on laws
of capillary motion
the contaminant chose its course

through her small body. Most of a layer
of skin and the fur
attached fell away all over the house
in ragged silken patches.
Lena's brother Eddie and even Isis –

Queen of Heaven, believer in magic,
lover of the downtrodden --
hissed at Lena and shunned
her for weeks while she stank of death.

But she did not die. She survived
to find chrysalides
everywhere, to bask
in baskets and crocks and barrels,

wooden bowls, clefts
between earth and stone walls,
leaf nests and brass kettles
for years of sultry afternoons.

All her former beauty was restored
and as soon as she smelled like life
again her family had no memory of fearing
her and she had no memories to forgive.

Wendy Merrick Burbank's *writing has been published in*
Naugatuck River Review (finalist, 2013 poetry contest), the
Narrowsburg River Reporter Literary Gazette, and Fed1a: a
digital display of ideas and information, and heard on the
Conflict of Interest Theater Company Podcast. Her poetry is

forthcoming in Armchair/Shotgun and Minerva Rising. She has been a featured writer at: Caffe Lena in Saratoga Springs, NY; BoCoCa Arts Festival in Brooklyn; and Catskill Mountain Foundation Center for Literary Arts. She lives and writes in the Helderberg Mountains in upstate New York and works on a large farm in the Schoharie Valley. (wendy.burbank@gmail.com)

London, My Friend Forever

By Maylin Carretero

Our first encounter involved a ditch by a street in my neighborhood. She was surrounded by children who, mockingly, shouted with sadistic encouragement,

"Come on, Rocking Chair, get up."

The dog was a skeleton of gray skin, a wolfish muzzle, drooping ears, and a cord like tail.

She struggled to rise with a little dance, twisting the front of her body, and then the rear half, until she achieved enough leverage to remain standing. She walked slowly. When the children's "diversion" was over, they ran off.

I approached Rocking Chair, the children's cruel nickname. I saw she was a female, about a year old, without a single hair, due to mange, that would reveal her color. Her eyes were black pits, full of despair.

I ran home to get food and water. When I returned, she had not moved. When she smelled the food and saw the water, she couldn't decide whether to drink or eat first, ending up doing both at once. Later, she followed me to the house, taking cover under the hedge lining the sidewalk. I set a bowl full of water next to her, and she fell asleep.

When my husband got home from work, I described what had happened, and he joined me when I fed her. I placed the food right next to her so she would not have to get up. We both recoiled at her condition. Although our home had ample gardens and yards, we already owned six dogs: two large dobermans, and four strays picked up from the street, as well as, three cats, also rescues.

In Cuba, there were shortages of all types, particularly food. It was quite difficult to maintain the animals we already had, so adding another one was unthinkable. Thus, we decided to nurse her to health, with the hope that someone would eventually take her.

The days went by. She improved, and I was able to inject her against mange and deworm her. One morning, when I came out to feed her, I didn't see her, and a neighbor reported seeing her walking down the street. I had been feeding her twice a day because of her malnutrition, and I decided to wait until the evening meal, convinced that she would return hungry. But she didn't return, and so the next day I went looking for her, particularly since my neighbor had alerted me:

"Those criminals who pick up dogs are out there...I saw their truck go by and there was a commotion just around the corner."

I ran looking for her with my heart pounding. Cuba has no laws for the protection of animals, and there is a section of the Public Health Department that is in charge of picking up stray dogs and "disposing" of them.

Finally, I saw her limping in my direction with the accursed dogcatcher's truck on her heels. I ran to her side and picked her up. They stopped, but after I gave them a stern look, they did not dare get out of the truck, well aware of how everyone despises them.

"You got away, you filthy thing!" they yelled mockingly.

40

I took her home and she remained in her shelter, safe for now, as the dogcatcher's truck would not come again for a while. Luckily, they are frequently short of gas for their work.

Two or three days went by and she was again feeding and resting. I spoke to and caressed her frequently, and I could see the expression of gratitude in her eyes whenever I approached.

A hurricane was approaching, and she again disappeared. This time I didn't wait and went looking for her all over the neighborhood, concerned how she would cope with the wind and rain. By the third day the fury of the hurricane struck. My anxiety was so great I took to the streets braving the wind, whistling and clapping as I always did to call her. On return, a neighbor told me that she had seen her return to her shelter under the hedge, in bad shape and very wet. She said that she had called to me, but I guess I had not heard her because of the wind.

I looked under the hedge, and there she was, shaking and unresponsive. My husband and I placed her on top of a burlap sack so that we could move her. We set up a tent in the carport, with blankets inside, with the back wall serving as a shield to the wind and rain. There we gave her sweetened warm milk with a spoon, dried her, and removed all the mud from her body. She opened her eyes, and I brought some warm food, which to our surprise, she devoured, followed by a lot of water. She laid down on the blankets, and quickly fell asleep in the well-protected tent.

Three days later, after eating well and sleeping, she seemed recovered. We removed the tent, and we saw that her skin was healing nicely. And so, after a good bath, we decided to leave her in the garden with Panfilo, Alegria, and Machucha, three lively and friendly dogs, previously rescued just like her. As the weeks went by her fur grew, and so did she, becoming a very beautiful dog with a handsome head, erect ears, thick legs, and the tail of a fox. The newly grown fur was orange/brick in some areas, and silvery gray in others, with the unusual finding that the distal half of each hair was a brilliant black, an unusual spectrum of shades. Her eyes were now dark walnut, with tints of loving honey. She would readily approach me, and I caressed, hugged and played with her.

Because of her startling beauty and the way she had entered my life, I decided to call her London, in honor of Jack London, my favorite writer of unforgettable dog stories. At times, I sat on the porch reading, and London would lie by my side, placing her head on my legs or feet. She never missed a chance to display her love.

One day, a good friend who lived in a nearby neighborhood, visited us. His wife, a doctor, was frequently on call at night, and he, himself, traveled a lot, leaving their son, age 14, alone. Even though they owned a nice home, well fenced, the rise in crime throughout the country had them worried. They asked if we would please gift them London, or at least lend her to them, until they could find another dog to provide safety and companionship for their son.

I was reluctant, because I was very attached to her, but the following day our friend came back, bringing his wife and son, all of whom became enamored of her. They were very insistent, supported by my husband who pointed out that this was an opportunity for London to be the sole mistress of her home, with a family who loved her, while providing safety and companionship to their son. Finally, the next day, I took London to their home, where I became satisfied that this would be an ideal place for her.

I reminded them that London had suffered greatly as a stray, and that she could never cope with returning to the streets. The parents and the youth swore to me that they would never allow her to run away. They pointed out, and I saw for myself, that their place was secure and she could not escape. Assured, I left her with them, and subsequently checked regularly on her. They always reported she was doing well, she slept with their son, and that she only went out with them to the backyard, enclosed by a wire fence.

Later that week, however, I was awakened by an uneasy feeling early in the morning. I had been missing London, and although I knew she was well, would break into tears when I came out and saw the little red doghouse she had appropriated when she was with us. That morning I came out to the porch with a cup of coffee. London! The cup fell from my hands, and I collapsed in a sitting position at the edge of the porch.

She was there, inside her red house! She approached me howling, crying, rubbing her head against me, and I picked her up sobbing. The noise awoke my husband, who was equally amazed that she had cleared the door on our fence, and a similar barrier to escape from our friends' house, while managing to orient herself to cover the three kilometers that separated us.

"I swear to you, London, my beloved dog," I said as I hugged her looking at my husband, "never, never will we be separated again."

And so it was. London and I were never separated. We had become friends forever.

Maylin Carretero resides in Havana, Cuba, and has a graduate degree in Language, English and North American Literature from the University of Havana. She is the author of AMIGOS PARA SIEMPRE, 2014, Alexandria Library, Miami, in Spanish, already translated into English, awaiting publication in English. She was the writer for children's programming on National Cuban Radio, and has been a member of the Union Nacional de Escritores y Artistas de Cuba (UNEAC) since 1981. Maylin is also the Founder and Vice President of the Asociacion Nacional para la Proteccion de Animales y Plantas (ANIPLANT).

My Little Rescue Friend

By Ada Chapman

I'm all alone. The room is cramped with barely enough space to move. Why are all these people staring at me through this glass? They tap on the window. It's making me nervous. And the weird smell in this room. But I am curious. Who are all those people? No, no, I just want to go home. But I have no home.

I think those are the thoughts that must have been going through the little kitten's mind as we and many other potential adoptive families gazed at her. There was quite a crowd at the pet store the day we first caught sight of the kitten who would become our cat, Pumpkin. I didn't know at the moment that I wanted a cat, let alone a rescue cat. It was a moment that changed my life. The moment I woke up to the fact that there were so many abandoned animals in our community, the day we welcomed home a new family member. I never thought rescuing an animal would be so rewarding and so life changing.

It was a chilly October afternoon. We were on our way home when I asked if we could stop at the pet store to look at the pets. My parents agreed. As we entered the store I smelled the musky smell of the fish water, bags of pet food, and other pet supplies. I saw many different pets up for adoption like cats, dogs and guinea pigs. We walked over to look at the cats first. I saw some tabbies, some spotted, some striped and some multicolored cats. Then, one of the tabby cats caught my eye. She was rolling around the cage and mewing and tapping on the glass with her small paws. There were people looking at her while she meowed from inside her tiny cage. The people were murmuring and whispering to each other. I thought they might be asking each other, "Can we have that cat? Aww! Isn't that cute? Can we please have a cat?"

Although I couldn't hear her, I just knew what she was thinking. She was an orange tabby who was only about nine months old. She had beautiful dark orange stripes interspersed with her light orange fur. She sat at the window of her tiny cage-like room and meowed. She tapped the cold glass window with her nose. I tapped the glass back to her. I thought she was adorable! All of my siblings thought so, too. All of the other cats and kittens were cute, but in my mind I knew she was the one. It was at that moment that I said to myself, "Ooh, I so totally want that kitten. I need a tiny best friend!"

My parents told me that she was a rescue from Lake Haven Animal Shelter. Someone—we will never know who—had found her with her mother and siblings outside in the cold. They were living at the animal shelter when they brought her to the store with the hope she would find a forever home.

I felt sorry for her, her mom, and her siblings. I wanted to adopt her so much that it was hard to think about anything else. She did many cute things and it was hard to think nobody else wanted her. My sisters and I were peppering my parents with questions: "Can we get this kitten? Isn't she super cute? Will you let us get her? Please? Please? Please?" I was super nervous about how my parents would reply. I really wanted her to come home with us. When my parents said yes, that we could get her, I was so happy I could have screamed.

My sisters and I worked hard to keep our squeals inside ourselves. I was so excited I couldn't breathe. We didn't expect to come home with a cat. She was just the purrfect cat!

I didn't know owning a cat would be so fun. Before I ever got Pumpkin, I thought a cat would just sit around and be lazy. I thought she would dose off each time I tried to play with her, to take catnaps all the time. But Pumpkin is more fun than I ever imagined. After we got her home, we discovered she loved to play and to be brushed. She can purr like the wind. She is so funny when she rolls on her back. Sometimes she rolls so much she bonks herself on the back of a chair or the table. She slaps at the curtains when she is trying to climb in the window. And boy is she curious! She sticks her cute little nose into everything. She may be small, but she makes a great big difference in our home.

Having a rescue cat is an entire world I didn't know about, and it changed my life (and Pumpkin's, too.) Having a rescue in my home and loving it has altered how I think about animals and people. All creatures are special in their own way. No animal deserves to be abandoned. And when they are abandoned, bad things can happen to them. They can get hit by cars, get hurt, be killed, and other bad things. I love having Pumpkin around. She's changed my whole life. Since my family rescued Pumpkin, I have become involved in cat rescue. This summer I went to a cat training class at my local humane society, and now I am a member of their Junior Volunteer Club. I will never know why people can be so cruel to animals, but I am ready to tell the whole world about the importance and rewards of adopting a rescue cat.

Teen author **Addy Chapman** *has long been an avid animal lover and an enthusiastic writer. This is her first published* story, although she hopes it will not be the last. When Addy isn't writing she spends her time caring for her own pets or volunteering. Her main interests are saving rescue pets, responsible pet ownership and fresh water marine biology.

Taking Chances

By Andrea Collins

I've seen a lot of ugliness, truly memorable saddening and unsavory living beings, like Dodger, a former Pit Sisters rescue dog. I discovered him in the middle of a busy road, emaciated, unnaturally hairless, with a child's belt hanging from his scabbed neck while drivers honked their horns and screamed at him to move out of their way. Many stray dogs in my neighborhood like Maggie, a basset hound, and our first rescue here in Jacksonville, Florida who was roaming playfully and eating trash in the streets near our home, surely faced similar health ailments and starvation had we refused to rescue and adopt her out to a loving home. If my wife and I lacked compassion, or possessed the fortitude it must take to look the other way, thereby ignoring the glaringly obvious suffering in our streets, then all 50 (or more) dogs that we have either rescued and fostered on our own, or transported to animal control for their own safety would know the misery and pain that Dodger once knew standing amidst a panorama of callous and impatient humans desperately wishing that he had never wandered into their direct vision, pissed off that they were forced to see ugliness normally concealed by their own blind fears and dispassionate thinking processes.

Often, I think of all the things I have not seen, like the backyard Dodger must have fled, trash and feces filling up his vision twenty-four hours a day. I think about what life was like for Mira, another dog on my block that my wife and I stopped to check on when we saw her cowering underneath a truck while her suspected owner lurked nearby. I wonder about the pain of those deep, raw, seeping wounds around her neck. I imagine she was pulled, strangled, and beaten by her owner while tethered to a cord that ripped into her skin like knife to butter. I wonder how she must've spent most of her two years of life gnawing on wood and steel chains attaching her to a post inside that backyard. Pit Sisters confirmed that she was nearly toothless when they rescued her from animal control. I consider the Miami dogs Pit Sisters rescued that were confiscated when it was discovered they were being used for bloody sport called, trunking. I wonder how terrified they must've felt being thrown into the trunk of a car by their caretakers. How dark and confusing not only their space, but their minds must have been. How unbelievably anxious and frenzied they were when they realized that another dog, likely their sibling, was already inside the trunk waiting to end the terror by ripping each other's throats out. All the grotesque and horrifying images of their lifetimes—their yard mates with their faces mutilated, their mothers, fathers or pack members with their eyeballs torn, ears shredded, tails bent, legs bro-ken—fill my nightmares. I cannot help but wonder about all they have not seen while surrounded by the ugly scenes they were forcibly thrown inside.

When I first met Lilli, a pit bull mix, I was only casually ac-quainting myself with her as a volunteer transporter for Pit Sisters. I was asked to pick her up from a shelter and bring her to an animal hospital for an assessment of her cancerous tumors. Having seen many deplorable images, and experi-enced plenty shocking and emotional rescues, I was ready for how she would appear. She was sickly, skinny, hairless, drooping nipples and vulva from overuse after innumerable litters, a sullen and lowly swaying head. The large tumor hanging from her abdomen, made her already worn and primitive features resemble a goat-like shape. As I stared at her while in the waiting area I wondered where in the world she gained the strength to smile so widely, full of eagerness and gladness, after I placed her in the back seat of my car. Where does she get the guts, the will, and the energy for such child-like vibrancy in her eyes?

She was a heart-worm positive, older gal, 10-years-old at least, and riddled with unknowable health issues. Yet she stunned me with her peppiness and her excited inquisitive explorations of the waiting room windows that she met with her nose. She appeared not to comprehend the images she was witnessing: the newness of doorways and reflections of cars and grass and trees cascading through the translucency of glass must've been overwhelming and thrilling. I could tell she enjoyed her discoveries of chair legs, as she sniffed them and rubbed up against them, and then sniffed them again. Intuitively, I knew she was seeing for the first time in her life a world of her dreams, and nothing, not cancer, worms, arthritis or fatigue, could keep her from experiencing all she was kept from throughout her former years of life.

Lilli must've been pleased when she was finally dumped out of a moving vehicle in front of a home where the residents would keep her in their back yard until Animal Care and Protective Services came to pick her up. She must have been delighted to, at last, be freed from whatever kind of hell she had been suffering up until the day she was abandoned on a suburban street. She must have had the foresight to know that being left on the side of the road was better than being imprisoned inside a breeder's filthy kennel, where I imagine all the abuses to her body took place.

I see, as if in cinematic motion, Lilli being placed inside a bathtub, two men holding her down, while another uses a small pair of pruning shears to mutilate her ears so badly that when you look down at her you can see directly inside her ear canal. I watch as they shove her face into the cold ceramic tile and chop her tail to the quick, so that the remaining nub barely covers her anus. I hear her squirming without a whimper or screech, shivering like she does when I bathe her. I see her being so brave and stoic while they grind her front teeth with a large metal file. She waits for these violent actions to end. She dreams of more than being used for her body to give birth to other dogs that will either know her same torturous experiences or know another kind of horror—like being starved and beaten until mentally strained enough to viciously attack a dog like her, helpless and passive, gentle and serenely imaginative. Lilli had to instinctively realize her stay at ACPS either meant a better kind of captivity or a means to a complete end to the life she left behind, but unexpectedly, her stay there meant something entirely different.

A worker at the shelter saw in Lilli what I saw the day I met her, and instead of listing her on a timeline for euthanasia, this person called Jennifer Deane, President of Pit Sisters, a non-profit organization dedicated to rescuing and locating loving homes for the most misunderstood dogs. Jennifer then saw what the worker saw: an exuberant will and a peaceful freedom fighter. She knew what I know, too: Lilli deserves to experience love and comfort, grass and sand, onion weeds and dandelions. She deserves to feel the sun warming the bare spot on her back, her newly grown white hair sparkling and gleaming as her smiling face reflects from the glass of my back door. Lilli wants to know everything that I know for certain, good people like Pit Sisters take chances on elderly, sick pit bulls. Passionate and kind people maintain a holding place for the happiness of those unlikely to survive. True champions of animal rescue sign their names on shelter adoption forms as caretakers of those dogs least likely to be adopted, most likely to die before they've even had the opportunity to truly live.

After several surgeries, for spay and to remove a 6-pound tumor from her abdomen, breast cancer, and a growth from inside her upper lip, Lilli has emerged from darkness, her flashlight of joy shining on a world I'm so happy to know with her now. As her foster, there is no greater, no more emotionally and spiritually inspiring experience than those flashes of jumping white as Lilli chases after me in the backyard. Her gummy, slobbery kisses on the side of my face when we take a ride on our way to our walking destination bring me a kind of joy that I, too, am newly embracing. Just knowing her, I feel encouraged and courageous. When I set my gaze and my mind on all that Lilli has seen, I feel empowered to make my own dreams come true, even when they seem so unachievable or improbable. I'll take my chances, too.

***Andrea Collins**' work appears in Apeiron Review, Beach Unleash, Bridge Eight, Matter, Off The Rocks, and Ash & Bones – forthcoming, Plath Profiles. A writing instructor for Ashford University, Warrior Writers, and Left on Mallory, and avid volunteer for Pit Sisters, she is grateful for all opportunities to combine her passions for writing and animal rescue by writing poetry, essays, and short stories about the animals she has rescued and fostered. Andrea earned her MA from Antioch University Midwest and her BA from Wittenberg University. http://pitsisters.org/*

Get Lost

By Linda Converse

Part One

It all started with Dino, the tiny grey kitten who came in through the cat door and immediately made himself at home. He climbed onto my chest at night and settled down with a steady purr while my big black tomcat, Kitten, looked on in disbelief.

This little guy was the start of an angst filled period in my life. My husband Rich and I were moving to a place that only allowed two animals. We already had our African Grey parrot Valentine, and Kitten. Dino could not come with us.

No one in the neighborhood knew where Dino came from, nobody wanted him, and all the no-kill shelters were full. Finally, I called the county animal shelter. They said that if he was "adoptable," they would do all they could to find him a home. So trusting their word, I picked up Dino as he purred innocently and put him into the cat carrying case for his ride to the shelter.

The county shelter was reputed to be a dreary, under-funded place and, in fact, it fit the description, but the two employees there seemed warm and caring. Rich and I took Dino out of the car and into the shelter. Before we knew it, he was being whisked off to a cage. Feeling quite guilty, I went over to his cage while Rich signed papers. Dino sat there with a dead expression in his eyes and he wouldn't come over to be petted through the bars. I had betrayed him. I felt sick.

The shelter chose certain animals to highlight with video clips on their website. After a few days I got up the courage to look at the site and there he was, walking around rubbing his face on the cage. That was when I found that they had given him the name Dino. A great description, based on what we'd told them, accompanied the video and I kept my fingers crossed that he would find a home. But I was afraid to check back to see what happened.

Dino's fate, and his dead expression, kept nagging at me, so one night I forced myself to look at the website. There under the "Happy Tails" of adopted pets was Dino. Phew! What a relief!

Part Two

Within days, however, a delicate, emaciated cat showed up. Was this Dino's mother looking for him, we wondered? This cat was frightened and distrusting. Again, no one knew who she was, and this time I knew her fate. She would not be "adoptable." I didn't think we could even catch her to take her in if we wanted to. But now what? If we started feeding her, who would continue after we moved?

I knew we couldn't let her starve, so I made a decision. I would make her adoptable. Rich didn't want to participate, so it became my job. We had a suspicion she was coming into the kitchen and eating Kitten's food during the night. During the day she hid under our car in the shade and watched me closely as I left ice water out for her nearby.

We put dry food out on the deck for her and moved Kitten's food into our bedroom. After about a month she started sneaking in while I was reading in bed at night and jumping up on the window ledge in our bedroom to get to Kitten's wet food. If I so much as moved, she'd bolt. But if I stayed still, she'd eat frantically, watching me the whole time, until she'd had enough, then race out. Some nights I'd get up to go the bathroom and almost get knocked off my feet as she streaked by in the dark.

One night I tried putting my hand out to her as she made her way across the bedroom. She stopped, tentatively put her nose to my hand, and then proceeded on her way to the food. We'd made a connection!

As she began to fill out, her unique appearance and beauty became evident. Her coat was tan, specked with short black hairs. A black line, exactly centered, ran down her tail to form a black tip. The undersides of her feet were black as tar. Her ears stood up in points and her green eyes stared out from her delicate face. She had the look of a tiny wild cat.

Unfortunately, Rich and I were not in agreement. While I was encouraging her to trust me so that she would become adoptable, Rich was telling her to GET LOST when he caught her sneaking down the hall to our bedroom. When I saw her looking at me wistfully through the cat door at night, I talked to her, encouraging her to enter, but Rich told her to scat.

As winter came on, the cat we now called Get Lost started sleeping at night on the chair by the woodstove and racing out the minute we woke up. I noticed Rich had stopped telling her to leave, but her name stuck with her. While I was gone for a week, he started putting wet food in the kitchen for her and he put a soft pink blanket on the couch where she now slept at night. It hadn't taken her long to win him over.

By the time I returned, she was sleeping on the couch next to Rich while we watched TV in the evenings. Soon she'd moved to my lap where she purred loudly as she let me scratch and pet her. She was becoming adoptable. Now I could truthfully say this would be a wonderful cat for someone, I began trying to convince people to take her, while wishing I could keep her for myself. The county animal shelter had merged with a larger one and when I called to inquire about their policy on euthanizing, they wouldn't guarantee me anything.

Finally a no-kill shelter agreed to advertise for me if I kept her in the meantime. But they said she needed to be spayed and have shots. So the next morning I left her at the vet for the day. Within an hour the vet called to say that she had a surprise for me—Get Lost was a boy, not a girl, and he had already been neutered. And, he was a purebred Abyssinian.

Figuring this wasn't a stray; I went straight to Google and entered "Abyssinian cat lost in Redding, Ca." Within seconds I had a lead - www.lifewithcats/TV had posted a story describing the following:

Res Q Animal Coalition of Redding, Ca. announced on September 24, 2012, the rescue of several semi-exotic and pure bred cats who had sat caged in a shelter for a year (while their legal status was in limbo) after being seized from a kitty mill operator...the beautiful Abyssinians, Bengals, Oriental Shorthairs and a Persian...came from a horrible situation and were now being readied to live normal lives.

And there on the website were pictures of cats looking just like Get Lost.

I left a message at the Res Q Coalition and later that day I received a call from a shocked woman named Janie who confirmed my suspicion. Yes, they were missing one of their

Abyssinians. He had escaped from his cage and she had been advertising everywhere—Craigslist, signs on telephone poles, the newspaper, but she had pretty much given up after three months. If this was the same cat, she said, she would have to take him back as he was being treated by a local vet and he wasn't yet cleared for adoption.

How this cat had gotten six miles from Janie's house to ours was a mystery.

Meanwhile Get Lost was nowhere to be seen after his harrowing ride with me to the vet. I told Janie I would call her as soon as he came in, if he did. Several hours later he came sneaking down the hall to the back bedroom where he hid behind a chair.

Soon Janie and her husband were here to pick up this cat that we, yes we, had grown very fond of. Poor Get Lost seemed resigned when Janie gently picked him up and soothed him as she carried him out. Here I go again, he must have thought. My husband called after them, "Will you let us know when he is adoptable?"

"Rich," I said, "What are you talking about?"

Not too long after this, I received a nice note from Janie. She wrote: "Xander just went to the vet and has been cleared for adoption. His fecal tests were totally negative! Yeah! Thank you so much for everything you did for him."

I stopped in several times at the Res Q thrift shop to inquire about Get Lost, aka Xander. Several weeks later I was thrilled to hear he had been adopted into a wonderful home and his new mom said he was a great cat. A young boy, who happened to be there with his mother, a volunteer, proudly explained that Xander was named after him.

The Res Q Coalition had accomplished what they'd set out to do before Xander took a brief side trip to our house, and I was, once again, happy and relieved. Not bad, I thought, two cats placed in six months—Dino and now Xander.

And, best of all, Get Lost was no longer lost.

Linda Converse *lives in Northern California with her husband, cat and African Grey parrot. She received a graduate degree in social work in 1977. The rich human experiences she was privileged to share through her work have deeply influenced her writing. Now retired, she enjoys pet sitting, writing and taking classes.*

Linda has been published in the Lost Angeles Times, the Chicago Tribune, La Joie Journal, Portfolio North and the New Social Worker Magazine. She self-published a book, She Loved Me, She Loved Me Not: Adult Parent Loss after a Conflicted Relationship in 2001.

A Good Old Buddy

By Deb Cusic

Several years ago, on a cold winter night, I was just leaving my mom's house for the evening. We had a good arrangement— she cared for my two dogs while my family and I were at work and school, and I helped her since she was 86 and suffering from health problems.

I was just loading the crew into my car when her neighbor came over. "Glad you're still here, Deb. We found this dog and don't know what to do. My husband says we can't have another dog."

I went over to their house and saw a long, furry little dog who seemed quite scared. With his gray muzzle and cloudy eyes, he also seemed quite old. His extra-long toenails clicked on the linoleum when he tried to walk. His fur was matted and he reeked of cigarettes. I was at my husband's limit of two dogs, Chloe and Scruffy, both terrier mixes. I figured I would have to take him to a rescue. But a thought occurred to me...

"Mom! Look at this!" I explained Buddy, as the neighbors were calling him for lack of another name, was wandering in the cold; and how when they brought him inside, he stood still for a while, as if frozen. Always having had a heart for a dog in need, my mom said, "He can stay here with me, just for the night." And those were famous last words, as it became two nights, three nights, and when it was clear all of our efforts at locating the owner were futile, the rest was history. Our only doubt was the dog door, which was a problem because my mom, recovering from a broken hip, couldn't make it down the porch step to open the actual door. "I can't keep this dog if I can't let him outside," she said. So we found a pole in the garage so she could reach the dog door to open it, so Bud would see how to get out. We took him to the vet, had cysts checked and rotten teeth removed, and asked the vet how old he was. The answer: "Pretty old, alright." But Mom delighted in his company and actually seemed thrilled to have her own dog, who didn't have to leave every night, although Bud didn't quite understand, and often tried to follow my two out the door. He soon settled in for the night, using his steps to get on the bed, since his little wiener dog (we think that's part of his make-up) legs couldn't make the jump.

So Buddy became a beloved family member, fitting in perfectly with my dogs to form the "Three Muttketeers." Buddy also had a career as a humane education dog. As a volunteer for the Humane Society of West Michigan, I would take Chloe and Scruffy to youth programs, schools, and even detention centers to talk about compassion and responsibility using the topic of animals. Joining the pack, Buddy quickly inspired compassion from many kids and teens, who sympathized with his missing teeth, lumps and bumps, and difficulty seeing. His story was a living example of neglect when we covered issues such as animal cruelty; yet also resilience as he quickly became a happy and loving dog when shown kindness. Although he never learned any cool tricks like my other two, the kids learned he wasn't valued for what he could do, but valued just for who he was. On a sad day a year later when Mom finally succumbed to her illnesses, Buddy came home to live with us.

We were faced with the challenges of an older dog sooner than usual after adopting one. Disorientation and loss of bladder control proved both sad and frustrating. But love doesn't give up; love is patient, kind, and understanding. After all, if we're fortunate, we'll all be old one day. And as a therapy dog, Buddy provided unconditional love and snuggling to his favorite nursing home resident, by being what she called her perfect lap dog. His presence even inspired my Girls on the Run team: although he could not keep up with them running like Chloe and Scruffy, they delighted in pushing him in his stroller.

Some people wonder why we would adopt an older dog, whom we would have for such a short time. Some people say he was incredibly lucky to have a second chance at a loving family. I think the opposite is true—we were blessed to have Buddy in our lives; no matter the challenges, no matter how little time we had together. Although the sadness of his loss is still painful, we take comfort in the memories of his sweet little spirit and hopes of a reunion at the Rainbow Bridge.

Deb Cusic *has been a social worker for 24 years, and currently works at Grand River Preparatory High School in Kentwood, Michigan. She and her dogs serve as humane education volunteers with the Humane Society of West Michigan, and have been involved in many different therapy dog adventures. Besides hanging with her canine buddies, Deb can usually be found playing basketball, roller blading, reading, skiing, and travelling with her family. She lives in Kentwood with husband Ed, son Marcus, and dogs Chloe, Scruffy, and Snowball. She can be reached at debcusic@gmail.com.*

Big Boy

By Gina Devries

My sister Lori has rescued quite a few animals in her life. They just seem to end up in her path, like when she saw a car hit a cat on the country road when she was on her way to work. The car didn't stop, but Lori had no trouble pulling over and taking the cat to the nearest vet. The cat healed and gratefully owners were found so all ended well. I could go on and on about my sister's big heart for rescues and matter of fact, it would be a thick book, but let me tell you about her most recent.

It was a Tuesday morning in August when Lori talked to a friend who was missing her run away beagle. Lori said she would go check out the local humane society because, why not, that's what friends do. While a few streets away from the shelter, she got behind a pickup truck carrying what looked to be a happy black lab having a mid-summer ride. With his tail wagging and face to the wind it gave Lori the sense that the dog was enjoying the ride.

Well, it wasn't until the pickup truck turned down the same street that would bring you to the shelter that the light bulb went on and Lori thought, *Oh this can't be good.*

When she and the pickup parked, she hightailed it over to the couple in the truck. Hellos were exchanged, and my sister didn't waste any time asking if they were going to surrender the dog. The lady said yes, that he was old and although he wasn't sick, they wouldn't be able to afford any vet bills he would need with him coming on 12 years.

My sister Lori said her heart missed a few beats. Of course, I will say one of God's angels to animals spoke the words, "May I have him?" The couple, who were also surrendering a cat, had no trouble saying yes. They said his name was Big Boy and he had been a good dog. The word had is what Lori was going to change as she moved Big Boy to her car and gave the couple her phone number and a thank you.

Lori noticed fleas on the matted and dirty hair of the thin not-so-big-boy dog as he laid on her back seat with a blanket that Lori carries for her own dogs.

"Well the first thing that is in order Big Boy, is a vet check and bath to get rid of those nasty fleas," Lori said as she drove to her veterinarian with her happy smile already falling in love with her back seat passenger.

After a vet check and a bath, the flea-free clean Big Boy was introduced to Lori's pack—two white Bichons; Bailey, a rescue, and Kota, and an orange rescue cat named Jake. Then there was Jager, a Newfoundland, who was a rescue from a few years back. They accepted Big Boy with open paws as they all know their leader Lori is always helping their fellow canines.

Lori put up her new friend's pictures on Facebook and told the story of how he came to her. It was like seeing one of those makeovers where the first picture shows the subject all grumpy without a smile and then in the next picture, after all the attention, you see a much improved smiling human, but in this case it was Big Boy the dog.

I went to meet Big Boy the next week and was greeted by a very happy black lab who had adjusted well to his new home. I threw him a ball in the big fenced backyard and, much to Lori's surprise, Big Boy was thrilled to fetch and drop it back at my feet, not once, but many times. With his wagging tail and smiling face, Big Boy no longer felt old and useless. Why, I myself think Big Boy just thought his previous owners had given him his last pickup ride to a place where his angel picked him up and took him to dog heaven.

I am proud of my little sister Lori for all she has done for the many pets who have come across her path. She always follows through finding homes for those she can't take, and she volunteers at the shelter as time allows.

Big Boy is doing great. I do believe he looks younger and has put on a few much-needed pounds. Lori loves to tell stories about all the happiness Big Boy has brought to her home.

So a big thank-you to my sister Lori and all the others who give their heart and time to caring for the many rescues and for being an angel to our fur friends here on Earth.

__Gina Devries__ is the author of <u>Fishing with Faith</u>, published in 2014 which won the spiritual category in both the New York Book Festival as honorable mention, and Paris Book Festival as runner-up. Gina resides in Hudsonville, Michigan with her husband Doug, and their loyal dog Grizwold. Email Gina at ginadevries1@aol.com.

Bud-Boo, W-underdog

By Lori Dishneau

About 100 years ago, when my husband Bob and I were first married, pre-kid, new house, full of optimism and delusion, we thought it would be an excellent idea to get a second springer spaniel to keep our first springer spaniel company while we were at work during the day. Even though we were reasonably intelligent people, we had not yet figured out the first law of owning more than one springer spaniel, which is best expressed as S1 + S2 = C3 or roughly springer One plus springer Two equals Chaos cubed. In other words, it equated out to the energy equivalent of roughly 15 high-energy dogs.

We had inadvertently purchased our first springer spaniel, Lucy, from a puppy mill. An advertisement in the newspaper for English springer spaniel pups made no mention that they had roughly 45 puppies from which to choose. We didn't even know such places existed until we went to pick her out. We bought her anyway, even though we were somewhat horrified. One dog rescued from unsavory circumstances, we rationalized. But to balance out the karmic load of indirectly supporting a puppy mill, we decided to contact the Springer Rescue organization for our second dog. We also wanted a dog we didn't have to housebreak and closer to our first dog's age so he didn't irritate her by being a puppy.

Adopting a dog from an Animal Rescue group is only slightly less rigorous than undergoing an IRS audit! This is for good reason; bless the people who run these organizations. But to say we were unprepared is another understatement. After completing paperwork, only slightly less detailed than my first top-secret security clearance application, we had a phone interview with the local coordinator for the Denver Springer Rescue group. She asked several additional questions that weren't covered on the application and decided that we sounded like potentially good candidates and told us that we could go and meet the dog.

"I do have to warn you," she said. "The rescue mom is a little bit unusual." She didn't elaborate further. She gave us the address and we agreed to go meet Bailey the following Saturday.

We had seen pictures of Bailey and he was a fine-looking boy. We also knew his back story. He was just eight months old and had already been passed to two different owners. He spent all of his time in the backyard in his most recent home after the family had a new baby and decided they didn't want an energetic inside dog.

Exactly on the appointed date and hour, we pulled up in front of a nondescript suburban house. No sense in making a bad impression with the people standing between us and our future new pack member. If the home visit was anything like the written paperwork, we knew that we had better ooze responsibility and accountability.

We rang the doorbell and were greeted by a cacophony of barking from within. A kindly looking, if somewhat disheveled, woman opened the door. We could see a middle-school aged boy in the background herding a pack of exuberant barking dogs toward the hallway heading to the back of the house.

"Come in, come in!" She gestured toward the living room where Bailey had been cut out from the herd, corralled off, and was now eyeing us with a mixture of curiosity and suspicion.

"This is Bailey," she said.

No novices to dog behavior and preferences, Bob and I plunked ourselves down onto the floor so that we could meet him on his level. Bailey reached out a big hairy paw and placed it on Bob's arm, followed by a shy kiss to Bob's right cheek. He had us at hello.

Given what we came to know about Bailey much later, this was highly unusual. Bailey preferred women, didn't care for strangers, and wasn't prone to affectionate behavior towards men. He was a ladies man. But clearly he was one savvy dude and knew whom he needed to win over to be placed in his forever home. He gazed deeply into Bob's eyes. I'm begging you.

"Ahhh, what a good-looking sweet boy," Bob said. Bailey dropped his gaze—Mr. Demureness. Aw shucks.

"Are you familiar with his history?" asked Rescue Mom.

We listened politely as she recounted Bailey's life on the lam, including an Olympic-level high jump over a chain link fence. "That dog can fly," she said. She explained the reason for his red coat (spending so much time outdoors in the sun), and how he got on with the other dogs. This last piece of information was important to us since we wanted a friendly companion for Lucy.

"Go get Rusty from the bedroom," she directed her son who had joined us in the living room. "We have been working with Bailey since he has been with us during the past month." She ushered us into the kitchen. "Bailey has a habit of counter shopping," she said. "I use this to train the dogs not to jump

71

up on the counters." She produced a small electronic device and placed it on the counter top and slapped down a piece of salami. "Watch this," she said.

Bailey, clearly on his best behavior, looked on dispassionately and didn't take the proverbial bait, although not from lack of encouragement by Rescue Mom.

"Let me just show you then." She pressed a button on the electronic device, which emitted a high-pitched noise. Several distressed yelps went up from Rusty in the back of the house.

"Oh, here's Rusty now."

A beautiful male springer spaniel trotted up to receive our pats.

"Now, Rusty," said Rescue Mom, "used to be on the police force."

"Really," we said with interest.

"Yes, in fact, one night, he crashed through our picture window in the living room and subdued a criminal from Florida who was outside of our house."

Bob and I exchanged looks while Rescue Mom's son touched her arm.

"That's quite a story," I finally said. The rescue mom is a little bit unusual. We thanked her for letting us meet Bailey and made for the door.

A few weeks later, the Springer Rescue coordinator, delivered Bailey to our new house in Golden, Colorado, despite having been told by Rescue Mom that we were adopting Bailey as a security dog for our double-wide trailer. Clearly she was wise to the elaborate stories. She could see for herself that we didn't live in a trailer, and we reassured her we were not adopting him as a security dog.

After re-naming him Buddy, which later morphed into Boo-boo, Boo-man, Bud-man, Booster, we settled into a happy routine. Lucy accepted him without reservation and the two dogs became inseparable.

With two dogs in the household, getting our sod laid in the yard moved way up on the priority list. The landscape materials company delivered a massive pile of sheep and peat fertilizer the next weekend. We rented a rototiller, loaded up the wheelbarrow and went to work. The dogs also enjoyed the fertilizer and as soon as we let them out of the house, made a direct beeline to the pile to roll and feast on the delectable sheep yummies.

I led the fragrant dogs back into the house and shut them on to the outside deck above the garage until I could bathe them later. Bob was in the driveway, which was below the deck, shoveling fertilizer into a wheelbarrow as I re-joined him to load the second wheelbarrow. As soon as I stepped on to the driveway, I sensed something coming through the air behind me. Turning around and looking up, I saw him—Bud-Boo, W-underdog—flying through the air, having cleared the short railing around the deck in one momentous leap.

As if in slow motion, he sailed over my head, and landed and rolled on to his back on the driveway as Bob and I rushed over to him.

"Holy S**t, we've killed the dog in the first week," I cried. "Buddy, buddy, buddy."

After peeing on himself as a reaction to our distress, he rolled over, shook himself out, and looked at us as if to say, "What's all this fuss?"

Bob and I laughed in relief that he appeared to be just fine. After all, we had been told that he could fly. He was truly our Wonder Dog and it would be just the first of many miraculous, ill-advised, funny, bone-headed, wonderful things that dog would do until the end of his days.

Lori Dishneau *is an outdoor girl, animal lover, office jockey, skier, good cooker, bibliophile, mother, wife, friend, writer, traveler, hiker, biker, knitter, not a quitter. After growing up in the Upper Peninsula of Michigan and graduating from Michigan Tech University, Lori struck out for the west. Once she got to the Rocky Mountains (great skiing), she stopped and put down roots and has been living in Colorado ever since (32 years and counting). She lives with her husband Bob and faithful Coton Du Tulear named Magic in Castle Pines. She is honored to have been selected for this anthology.*

A Toast to Mr. Cranky Pants

By Patti Eddington

I'm off-kilter, these days.

My funny, obstinate, crabby kitty, Boz, aka The Fat Bastard, died recently.

I have the same tear-in-the-universe feeling everyone has when they lose a beloved pet. I expect to see his vast bulk stretched in front of the heat vent in our bathroom. I think I hear him stomping around the kitchen. I'm amazed when I open the door to the cat room and urine and feces are inside the pan.

So, I'm at odds and out of sorts.

I think my mood is about more than being one animal short. I think it's because for the last 40 years I have never been without a mean-ass rescue cat. We still have two cats but, against all odds, they are sweet and docile.

I got my first cranky pants kitty when I was 13, after my parents decided to sell my pony Susie, and her less than brilliant son, Star, without telling me. I was inconsolable. I cried for hours, phoned the Dial-a-Prayer number in the phone book hoping for divine intervention, then snuck to the barn in the night and whispered my plan into Susie's musty mane. I would take her and her ignorant offspring and we would escape, living in the woods, at least for a day or two, in hopes of bringing my parents to their senses.

"I love you, Susie, I won't let them take you away," I sobbed.

Susie snorted and tossed her hard head, smacking me in the nose, then stepped back planting her full weight on top of my sandal-clad foot.

"On second thought," I told my mom, "I'll understand if you sell them. But, could I get a cat?"

I got my cat in a "be careful what you wish for moment" while visiting Susie and Star at their new farm. They showed absolutely no sign of recognizing me, but I was consoled by the sight of a scrawny kitten, ignored and hungry, living in the haymow. I looked at my mother, she sighed, nodded slightly and the kitten was gathered into my cardigan and clutched tightly to my chest.

The resulting bloodstains came almost all the way out with the help of a little peroxide and cold water.

Toby evolved into a longhaired, orange and white beauty with a penchant for hanging on the back of the living room drapes and sitting for hours under our bird feeder.

"Eat the mice, not the birds, Toby," my mother would shriek out the front door. "The MICE, not the BIRDS!"

Toby would turn slowly to look at her, blink his yellow eyes and, ultimately, devour another sparrow.

He lived a long life, long enough to loathe J.P., the Siamese kitten my husband Jim, gave me for Christmas the first year we were married.

J.P. was the skinny runt of a litter Jim saw advertised in the classifieds. He drove his crummy Chevette 20 miles to a hash-house during a snow storm, and gave the woman $25 to rescue the little guy.

"I had to adopt him, Babe," Jim told me. "He was already inhaling."

Under our guidance, J.P. grew stocky and moody. He stalked around each of our five apartments and three homes growing progressively crabbier every year.

He lived to be 17 and his death sent me into an inconsolable tailspin, which might have gone on longer, except I met Boz.

Found in the middle of the main street of our village, he was hit by a car and left to die. We took him home and nursed him to health.

Boz lived his entire life as if he were a supremely naughty, 12-year-old boy. He ignored rules, back-talked, and ran away whenever he could. The escapes often went undetected and he spent many nights apparently strolling the neighborhood, and then batting at our backdoor at dawn demanding re-entry.

Jim eventually bolted our window screens to the house because Boz would use his immense girth to push them out and waddle off. My friend and neighbor, Cindy, called me one day while I was grocery shopping.

"I just drove by your house and your cat is sort of hanging out of your upstairs window. Do you want me to go in and get him down before he jumps or falls?"

Long pause.

"Patti?"

"I'm here," I responded. "I'm thinking about it."

He refused to urinate in cat litter, preferring the sheet of newspaper we placed under the pan. So, we began providing a pan with a sheet or two of newsprint just for that purpose. It necessitated me glancing surreptitiously around the grocery store, and then sneaking a handful of auto trade sheets, Home for Sale ads and supermarket supplements advertising: "Jif!

Assorted Varieties! 2 for $5!" when no one was looking. Then, I slipped quickly through the automatic doors, my heart racing a bit, my face placid to hide the elation I felt simply knowing that, for a few more days, my home was safe.

We put up with Boz and his foibles for 15 years.

Because that's what they really are, you know, just...foibles.

Toby ignored my Mom's "mice not birds advice," but on summer nights he would sit quietly beside her on the back porch of our farm house, gazing at the apple orchard, listening to Ernie Harwell call the Detroit Tiger games, and enjoy a small bowl of vanilla ice cream.

When people who knew J.P. learned I was pregnant with our daughter, Molly, they warned us we would have to "get rid of that mean cat." We didn't because it was never necessary. J.P. curled against Molly's baby carrier the first night she came home from the hospital and rarely left her side. He slept with his body pressed tightly to her baby seat and stood below the changing table like a sentry. In the days before his death, when his hip bones protruded at sharp angles and the only food he could eat was finely chopped turkey, I would search the house frantically for him and finally find him curled on her pillow.

And, anyone who really knew Boz, who heard him protest vehemently with a loud "squawk" whenever he was picked-up, knew it was simply a facade.

I don't plan to get another cat anytime soon. We are one cat down, but we are not out.

Still, I can't say never. Maybe someday someone will offer up just the right blend of fur, whiskers and ornery disposition and I'll be tempted.

I'll give it a lot of thought, though, knowing that in the best of all worlds, I'll have 15 years and then have to pull myself up from my puddle on the floor and lurch forward again. But, I just might say yes. I just might be waiting with open arms...and a welcome heart.

Epilogue:

His name is Symon Francis O'Toole, though he is often called O'Toole the O'Foole, and he was a badly-kept secret.

Sitting at Stan's, an atmospheric local dive, one night a few weeks after Boz died, my friends Sally, Betsy and I discussed what we wanted for Mother's Day.

"Well," I said. "I'm not sure I want it, but I have a feeling I'm getting a cat."

Sally gasped.

"Really?" I asked. "Really?"

"No, I don't know anything!" she yelped, turning quickly back to her Scotch.

It's odd, because Symon isn't a traditional rescue. Molly, paid $200 from a Siamese cat breeder and drove across the state to a dicey neighborhood—shades of Jim and J.P. 32 years earlier—to pick him up.

Molly saw little Symon in the musty, cluttered and chilly garage where he was being "raised," saw the breeder yank him, unkindly, from his mother as he nursed and realized he needed our help as much as Toby or Boz ever did.

Like his predecessors, Symon is sweet and obstinate. He is loving, ornery and strange. He has eaten an annoyingly large chunk out of our new living room couch and urinated (twice) on our favorite, expensive, leather chair.

For these sins, he has been reprimanded and, ultimately, forgiven. Since he is so young, it is a cycle which promises to repeat, for a very long time, if we are lucky, perhaps 15 years or more.

Patti Eddington *is a longtime former journalist living in Spring Lake, Michigan. Today, she works as Marketing Director for Harborfront Hospital for Animals and Veterinary Dental Solutions, and teaches dance fitness.*

She is married to James Moore, DVM, and the couple have one child, Molly, 23.

Her blog, "Don't Look in the Freezer, The Life and (Sometimes Strange) Times of a Veterinarian's Wife" can be found at dontlookinthefreezer.blogspot.com

She is honored her work is included in this anthology.

A Dog Mystery

By Harold Garrecht

It was early fall 1957 when I got an emergency telephone call at the Marine Base where I was stationed. It was my then pregnant wife Cathy, and she was in tears but very angry and agitated. After calming her down a bit she told me that a cop who resided across the street from us in the town of Edenton, North Carolina had just shot a dog that had recently given birth to several puppies.

The mother of the pups was a very friendly stray dog who took residence under a neighbor's house where she allowed the dog to take refuge. My wife cried because she had befriended the stray mother of the pups. Being an animal lover she wanted to keep the smallest of the litter. Her being an expectant mother of our first child and me being honorably discharged within a month after serving four years put an extra burden on us as we were expecting to move in with my parents until we could get our own place in the Bronx (NYC). Of course being a good guy and also an animal lover, I caved in to her wishes. We named the female pup Tina after her mother.

On March 15th, the day after my wife gave birth to our son Fritz, I took Tina for her daily walk around the block from the apartment where we then lived. It was a typical tenement apartment area with busy streets and plenty of cars and trucks. The frisky Tina was about seven-months-old and she could run. So that's just what happened. She wriggled out of her collar and leash and ran. The chase was on.

She was a wild thing and totally unaccustomed to the city. She was fast, very fast, and I ran after her for blocks. It seemed I was always a block away. I couldn't gain on her.

She thought it was a game when she looked behind to see if I was there and still coming. At one point I hailed a taxi, and we followed her north for at least two miles during which we tried several times to lure her into the taxi. It didn't work so the chase continued. I even left the cab without paying too, still chasing this black and white tail wagging terror when she went alley hopping in a very dingy area.

About two hours of chasing, calling, cursing, sweating, panicking, and swallowing my pride I gave up the chase when I completely lost sight of her. I returned home near tears as I looked at her collar with her name tag and our telephone number still attached. How do I tell my wife, who went through forty hours of tough labor, then a caesarian section during the birth of our son, that I had lost her precious puppy? She would be devastated.

How low did I feel? You're right, exhausted and about as low as slime under a snail.

It was early the next morning, about seven a.m., when a neighbor called and said that she thought our Tina was barking at the front door to our building.

"What? How? Tina? She found her way back? My dog returned? How could this be?" I ran and jumped down three flights of stairs. Yeah, there she was. I took deep breaths while near tears of joy.

Our Tina wagging proudly and barking as she saw me, "Well, I'm home, where did you go? Why did you leave me?"

To think I was stunned and amazed is putting it mildly. I couldn't even scold her. How could she have found her way back through alleys, vacant lots, and busy streets with cars, buses and trucks? She invented GPS, that's how. It's still a dog mystery of a welcome wonder that ended with a face lick and a hug. Wait!

This wonder didn't stop there. About eight years later, my wife's father was staying with us after recovering from heart problems. He was returning from a leisurely stroll when loud anxious barking caused my wife to open the front door. I heard her scream. I knew it wasn't because of Tina, or was it? Her Dad had just disappeared beneath a cesspool cave-in as he walked across our lawn. I ran to the collapse and peered into the deep. His hat was floating, but he was totally under the surface. I ran to the garage and retrieved a ladder as my wife dialed 911 for assistance.

My son and I put the ladder down into the mess, suddenly we felt and observed a hand grabbing on and we retrieved the old gentleman who was choking profusely but hanging onto the ladder. We cleared his mouth with fingers, washed his face with towels, and firm pats on the back helped to clear his throat somewhat. The ambulance and fire department arrived and they were surprised he made it and was able to breathe again. He was removed to the hospital where he needed a ten-day stay and a month in therapy to return to normal. What if my wife didn't open the front door when she heard Tina barking? What if Tina never found her way back eight years before? Was this a dog miracle? It sure is a dog mystery. Woof!

Harold "Harry" Garrecht *is a proud American and "Once a Marine always a Marine" who served as a Sergeant during the Korean War. Harris is also a long retired NYPD Sergeant and* *recipient of many Police Dept. awards. As a lifetime dog lover of many breeds, he has Riley from a pup that is now an eleven-year-old rescue from North Shore Animal League in Port Washington, NY. Dogs are a human's best friend, also. Harry's detective novel, <u>Passion and Desperation</u>, is available as an eBook on Amazon.*

How I Was Rescued

By Mary Aiello Gauntner

Years ago when I worked in a greenhouse, I stopped in one day to check and see when the plants would be coming in for planting. While looking around the greenhouse, checking out the plants, something round ran by my feet. Whatever it was, it startled me. I looked around and didn't see anything. Shrugging this off to my imagination, I walked to another part of the greenhouse. Before I knew it, resting on my shoe was the smallest black and white kitty, looking up at me and mournfully meowing at the top of its tiny lungs.

I leaned down and scooped up the meowing kitty. It just kept going to town, meowing. I looked at its green eyes and cuddled the cat under my chin, saying, "You are a sweet, little thing. Where did you come from?"

The little kitty snuggled closer, stopped meowing and began purring loudly. A co-worker heard me and responded, "That's a stray someone dropped off at the greenhouse the other day."

The kitty snuggled closer, stopped purring and licked my face. My co-worker continued, "That kitty likes to catch the mice that run through the greenhouses."

I pulled the kitty away and wiped my face with the sleeve of my sweatshirt. I held the kitty and it started to purr, again.

Laughing, I added, "So, he's the watch-kitty for the green-house?"

"He's the watch-kitty for the greenhouse," she answered. "Rich (the co-owner), hates cats. Bill (the other co-owner) is allergic to them. Rich is taking the kitty to the humane society after work."

My heart skipped a beat when I heard her say the humane society, knowing if they didn't find a home for the kitty it was history. Before I could stop myself, I said, "They can't do that. They can't just dump this kitty off at the shelter. If no one takes it, they will put it down."

My co-worker just shrugged her shoulders as if to say there is nothing I can do about it.

I looked at the kitty and it looked back at me. Without thinking I said, "I'll take it." I left and got into my car. On the drive home, the kitty sat contently on my lap and purred loudly the whole way home. At home, I pulled out a new litter box, filled it, and pulled down the cat bowls that had been washed and filled one with water and the other with milk. I made a mental note to buy kitty food as soon as I could.

Later as I sat in my rocker in my bedroom, the kitty jumped on my lap and sat there purring. There was something about this kitty that I liked. It turned out to be a female, and I named her Smudge, but one day while I was eating, she hit the roll out of my hand and I re-named her Scraps. Scraps loved to eat. Scraps loved to sit on my lap and meow. When I went to bed, Scraps would sleep at the foot of my bed, inching up until she nestled her head between my shoulder and arm. Then with her paws, she would pull my arm around her, all the while purring.

As time went on, Scraps really got bigger and fluffier. She also had asthma and would wheeze when she purred. Whenever I took her to the vet or groomer, I couldn't get her into the carrier. So, I would wrap a blanket around her and carry her that way. Scraps would put both paws around my neck like a baby. It was funny. It was cute. Oddly, it was comforting and soothing to both of us.

A few years later, my children were all grown and left the nest. Then my husband left, too. I was all alone, but I wasn't. For me, Scraps sensed my sadness and loneliness and was always there close by, following me around, sitting on my lap or sleeping on my shoulder. Scraps filled up the loneliness and emptiness. She filled up the empty side of the bed.

Seventeen years later, Scraps was still around, still eating, still as fuzzy as ever, still a part of my life. Then she got sick. The vet wasn't sure what was wrong with her. She walked with a limp like she had arthritis, a bit like me, her owner. When she couldn't jump up on the bed, I would pick her up and put her there. Sometimes she ate. Sometimes she seemed to have lost her appetite. I tried every type of food to feed her, but even the food I ate didn't seem to appeal to her.

Finally, I called the vet for another appointment. The night before the appointment, I held Scraps on my lap for a long time, just stroking her long black and white fur. That night she slept next to me on my bed with her wheezing/purring.

Somehow I knew that something more was wrong with Scraps. I hoped that it would be minor, but it wasn't. Scraps just lay quietly on the veterinarian's examining room table. She never purred, not once. She kept her head tucked between her paws. She never looked at me or anyone.

I gently bent my head down and touched the top of Scraps' furry head with mine, and quietly said goodbye to my faithful companion, who seemed to love me unconditionally. She was my favorite pet who always was there for me, under my feet, begging for food, sitting on my lap, lying by my head with my arm that she insisted I place on her neck.

I went home and broke down. I was shocked that I would cry for Scraps so much. This was just an animal, but she wasn't. I rescued her from the greenhouse, but I really didn't. She rescued me at the lowest point in my life and she kept me from drowning in my grief. Now I was grieving for her.

The next day I went into work in the greenhouse. In time, the owners had changed their minds and took in another cat to keep out the mice and chipmunks. The cat was a big yellow tabby named Tonka. I made a beeline for Tonka, who was sleeping in a basket. Tonka woke, looked at me and purred loudly as I started to pet him. I said, "You know, right?" The cat just purred louder as I petted him for a very long time. For the day, Tonka followed me into the greenhouse and laid on one of the benches as I planted, watching me and purring.

Tonka knew. Somehow Tonka sensed I was grieving. It was then that I fully comprehended that Scraps was the one who rescued me. I gave her a good life and she lived a long time, but Scraps really was my rescuer, as was Tonka on this day.

*As a mother of nine children, **Mary Aiello Gauntner**, has had her share of cats, turtles, gerbils, guinea pigs, rabbits, and fish.*

With a Master's Degree in Nonfiction Writing from Chatham University in Pittsburgh, Pennsylvania, she has had many articles in magazines and newspapers published. Having had two full length novels published, The Doctors' Wives and A Leap of Faith, she is currently working on a series of children's books. Working part-time at a greenhouse, babysitting for her grandchildren, and helping to prepare foods in her daughter's catering kitchen, provides her with lots of writing material.

Worm Crossing the Road

By Brian Gillie

"To be frank, I think you're wrong about our role on their behalf;
More bluster and contempt won't change the score.
Diplomacy's the way to get solutions back on track,
So we agree to disagree once more."
On morning walks our caffeinated minds are in high gear;
We're fresh from NPR and Morning Joe.
And undistracted I can make my politics quite clear,
But shoot, there's a worm crossing the road.

Today the early light parades its purples and its pinks,
Around this curve where amber fields rise.
Our eyes scan the horizon, but my stride is out of sync;
As usual, I'm too preoccupied.
For though I'd love to be at liberty to walk carefree,
Admiring all Mother Nature holds;
To elevate my soul with lines of song and poetry,
Back up! There's a worm crossing the road.

So, what's up worm? Your risky venture seems so random it's a
stretch to think you have a plan.

And if the heat on this dark pavement doesn't dry you out and turn you brittle black,

And if the rain-drenched soil doesn't force you to the curbside where an incidental puddle turns you flaccid pink,

Then it's for sure the heavy wheel of man's entitled drive will crush you, unobserved,

And all your perfect evolutionary parts will go for naught, right here, mere inches from the safety of your scrambled, moon-scaped dirt.

And when I kneel to coax you here into my palm...your wild, evasive squirming rivals convoluted highlights of a Chinese ribbon dance.

Too bad you are slimed and disagreeable for in a pleasant suit you might dazzle and be showcased in the family-room terrarium.

Instead...this day I will deliver five of you back to the safety of the garden by the shaded path,

And tomorrow...I will gather up another eight of your companions who will somehow think the road is their escape—or escapade.

So far this hot, mid-summer cul-de-sac has offered up one hundred twenty-three of you with radar gone awry,

Some baking in the heat, some helplessly submerged, some paralyzed, encrusted in the residue of salt and sand that tamed last winter's freeze.

I'm on your case...to sweep you clean of grit, to lifeguard by your puddle, and to lift you from the blacktop carefully...quite expert now at keeping bow and stern intact.

Amused and tickled by your worried squiggle here inside my fist, I bless your energy and tender your reprieve,

Accustomed now to serving as the eyes, the legs, the wings you would have used to orchestrate your own escape

Until at last...with winter you go deep, and thankfully I'm never
called upon to take my sympathetic fingers from the glove.

Next springtime, though, you slimy slitherers will take your leave
Of subterranean and foreign worlds;
Here once again emerging to this place that carelessly
Ignores your beauty under foot and wheel.
And you can't hide from robins who go searching in the rain,
Unearthing you like backyard rubber bands.
Hey, I admit you're needed at the bottom of the chain,
And for your sacrifice to Nature's plan.

Still, I'll politely nod on morning walks as I pretend
I'm all about the news and scenery;
And I'll apologize up front for rude indifference,
As I tune out with one eye to the street.
But worm, though you've no clue that I'm about to intercede
And change your course from squish or fry...to home;
Our thirty second friendship makes for oddball therapy:
Feels good...you and me, crossing the road.

Brian Gillie *is a teacher and performing artist with Connecticut Arts for Learning (formerly Young Audiences of CT) and the CT Commission for Arts and Tourism, specializing in the histories of American popular song and American social dance. Brian is also an accomplished percussionist, dancer, pianist and singer with a long history of group and solo performance from ragtime to hip-hop. Brian's special avocation is performing American songbook classics and '50s rock 'n' roll at venues throughout Connecticut. Contact Brian at bgillie48@yahoo.com.*

Waiting to Go Home

By Juley Harvey

i understand these rescued animals
in the no-kill shelters —
we don't fit in,
we're not all that pretty,
or cute or clever-witty,
or well-behaved or easily molded
or society's prizes —
one size fits all —
but we remember kindness
and it is a country
where we would dwell. be holded.
and repay those who offer it
with our furry lives, however big or small.
tiny things, perhaps,
but everything,
wrapped up in fuzz,
forgiving-wise,
a cuddly valentine forever-was.
if humans ever learned such stuff,
we could banish war and all the rough,
but we at the top of the food chain gang,
say who lives and dies and when and what for
and don't give a hang.

bloody valentines massacre.
ah, men! amen.
save yourselves, ladies —
rescue a fur.

Juley Harvey *is a former journalist (in both California and Colorado), and a prize-winning poet. Her poems have appeared in more than 35 publications. Most recently, she received a third prize in Dancing Poetry's contest and honorary mentions in the Estes Valley Library's Fire and Flood Memorial Poetry Contest, last year.*

Her poem, "waiting for the firestorm," has just been published in Outrider Press' black-and-white series, "Embers and Flames."

She lives with her faboo 5-year-old rescue, wire-haired terrier/Chihuahua, Moosie, at the gateway to Rocky Mountain National Park, helping her 94-year-young father, and dreaming of the ocean.

Getting Skunked

By Elizabeth F. Hill

Born Free it was not. The scenario that played itself out before our eyes was not the stuff of legend and would never feature in a film. No orphaned lion cubs to amaze, no captive whales to overwhelm; no loyal dogs to tug at heartstrings, no experimental species to outrage. Not even Canadians could be expected to watch a film without any big name stars like a moose or a bear—or at the very least a beaver or a blue jay. There was never any chance the movie cameras would roll. Nevertheless, despite its paucity of danger, intrigue, or pathos, it was, in its own way, a heroic rescue.

The drama unfolded late in an August afternoon on Mapleward Road, possibly the only route in all of northern Ontario that was not blocked by construction. We'd spent the day running errands in Thunder Bay and were on our way back to Lake Shebandowan. We were hot, tired, and eminently ready to relax, cold drink in hand, at our camp, only an hour's drive away. As my husband said, "We're going to camp, directly to camp. We are stopping for nothing, not even doughnuts at Tim Horton's."

That, of course, seemed a bit extreme, and like many a lofty aim, totally missed the net. We turned a corner and, not ten meters ahead; a big white pick-up was parked in the middle of the road, its hazard lights flashing, and no driver to be seen.

This was a bit strange—even for the north shore of Superior. We'd heard of people texting in their trucks, strumming guitars in their trucks, even barbecuing steaks in their trucks, but people didn't usually desert their trucks.

"So where on earth is the driver?" I asked.

"Probably answering the call of nature," my husband said.

"You're right, Dad!" our son exclaimed. "He's walking his cat!"

"His cat? Where?" we asked.

"Right over there. See that big cat? Wow, he's beautiful—all black with a fluffy tail."

We unrolled our windows to get a closer look at the young man and his cat.

"No, wait, he's not all black, he's also got two white stripes and a long white nose."

We hastily rolled the windows back up.

"Maybe we should back the car up," I suggested. "I don't want to be too close to this."

"Geez," our son said. "That stinks! Are we scared of one little skunk? That guy is right out there with it."

"One little skunk," I pointed out, "has an extremely accurate aim and can produce one mighty stink. Not for nothing are they called 'nature's perfume factory'."

"We are wary of skunks," my husband added. "It's okay to make room for these odious animals. Even Charles Darwin said so."

"I didn't know that skunks have long white noses," our son said. "And why's that guy hitting it with that stick?"

We looked closer. The skunk was sporting a plastic soft drink cup on his snout. Someone had evidently tossed the used cup in the bush for any opportunistic omnivore to find and imbibe. The skunk was now, as the saying goes, deep in his cups. The container was stuck fast on his face, completely covering his snout and his eyes. The young man, obviously a sensitive creature himself, was attempting (very carefully) to knock the cup off the skunk's head.

The difficulty for the youth was that the skunk did not appear to be convinced that he was being helped. Every time the stick touched the cup, the skunk would sense danger, turn his backside in that direction, and raise his tail. The young man was constantly jumping out of the potential line of fire.

The circle dance continued for at least twenty minutes. The youth would knock the cup, the skunk would threaten to put in his two cents' worth, and the youth would jump out of the way.

"That's eleven for the skunk, zero for the man," our son remarked.

At long last the cup fell off.

The skunk froze, looking long and hard at the young man. The young man backed up.

The skunk turned and ambled away into the bush. The young man picked up the cup and tossed it into the back of the pick-up. We gave him the thumbs-up and he nodded slightly. Then he got into his truck, turned off his flashers, and drove away.

Munching on a doughnut at Timmy's, our son asked if this is why we say someone is 'drunk as a skunk'.

"I don't think so," my husband replied. "But it's what I call getting the job done without raising a stink!"

Elizabeth F. Hill *holds a doctorate in intercultural education and has lived and worked on four continents. Her poetry has* *appeared in numerous publications, including The Haiku Journal, Feathertale Magazine, and Brain of Forgetting. She has co-authored one novel, <u>Love in the Age of Dinosaurs</u>, which was published by Uncial Press under the name of Sorcha Lang.*

A Forever Home for Foxy

By Lenore Hirsch

A red-haired dog lay under a leafy tree in the front yard of the house. A car stopped at the curb for a moment, slowly pulled away, then backed up and parked.

"This is the right address," said the woman as she noticed the dog disappearing around the corner. The couple rang the bell, listening to barking and howling from inside. The noise stopped as the door opened and they entered.

The dog, short-legged and pointy-nosed, peered around the corner from another room as they chatted with Margie, the foster mom. "This is Rufus," she said.

"He's just as cute as the picture on the Internet," the woman said. Rufus approached slowly and sniffed her feet, then the man's. They were both wearing tennis shoes with rubber soles.

"He's a sweetheart," said Margie, "but he's so timid the shelter couldn't find a home for him." Margie handed the lady a slice of bologna and the lady offered it. Pointed ears straight up, tail wagging, he grabbed it from her hand and scooted out of the room, gulping it down. The man asked if they could take Rufus for a walk.

Margie put on the leash and Rufus followed the two strangers out the door and down the sidewalk. The dog pulled and struggled to run ahead, crossing the sidewalk back and forth in front of the lady, who held the leash.

"Hey, sweetie, slow down," she said. "He's so cute, Jay, can we take him?"

"He isn't very friendly," he said, "and doesn't know how to walk on a leash."

"He just needs training," she said.

Back at Margie's, the people talked and then the couple took the dog out to their car. The woman picked him up and put him on the man's lap in the back seat. Jay held the dog while she got in front and started the car. The dog squirmed, then sniffed the fresh laundry scent on Jay's arms and legs and settled down a little. The car swayed and the dog felt a lump in his throat.

Jay started, "Ellie, I think he's going to--" The dog vomited all over Jay, but Jay held on.

"I can't stop yet," came from the front.

After a few minutes, the car stopped at a park and Jay lifted the dog out, putting him down on some grass. Ellie took him for a short walk while Jay found a place where he could clean up. Ellie offered the dog some water in her hands and they all climbed back in the car. Jay's clothes were wet and no longer smelled so good.

Finally they arrived at a condo. It was in a big complex on the ground floor, with neighbors on both sides and up above. Ellie led Rufus around the house on his leash, showing him the kitchen, the bedroom and an office. The dog sniffed everything. After a while, she took the leash off and he explored all the rooms, enjoying the feel of the soft carpeting under his feet and, when he finally lay down, under his belly. In the small yard behind the house he sniffed the scent of bay trees and heard water rushing in a nearby creek. After some evening kibble and a walk outside, Ellie put a soft cushion next to the bed and cooed at Rufus to climb on. She put a treat on the cushion and praised him when he retrieved it.

"That's my good boy. Good job!"

They gave the dog a new name. "Who calls a dog Rufus?" said Ellie. "He looks like a little fox, so let's call him Foxy."

At first, the couple did not leave Foxy alone in the house. If one of them went out, the other stayed behind. The dog followed Ellie around the house, but kept his distance from Jay. One day they both went out and closed the door. The dog sat by the door and barked. They came back inside. Every time they both stepped outside, he barked. One afternoon they got ready to go out.

"Ellie, are you ready? We're going to be late."

"Honey, I know it's our anniversary, but do you think it's safe to leave the dog?"

"We can't take him with us to the restaurant and we both need a break," he said. "We'll come back in an hour."

Then they were gone. Foxy sat by the door and listened to the humming lights and machines in the house. He barked non-stop, but they didn't come back. He barked louder. He jumped on the door. Soon he was panting and thirsty. Someone yelled from far away and he heard pounding through the wall. He continued to bark. Finally he heard footsteps and Ellie's voice. The door opened, he jumped up, wagged his tail in a 180-degree arc and ran round and round. Nobody else was smiling.

The next time they went out without him, Ellie left behind some treats in a rubber ball. He forgot to bark for a little while. After a few more times, he got so busy with the treats in the ball when they left that he hardly barked at all.

Life took on a routine. Ellie walked and fed Foxy in the morning, then left for the day. Jay sat in the office in front of a computer or watched TV. When he ate something, he gave Foxy a taste. Sometimes they walked to the neighborhood coffee hangout and sat at an outside table where he could lick crumbs from the sidewalk and greet other dogs who came to visit.

Later on, Ellie returned and after hugging both her guys went into the kitchen to cook dinner. Foxy stayed close by while they ate at the dining table, in case anything dropped on the floor. In the evening they all sat on the sofa, Foxy in between them; often one would stroke his head while the other massaged his back.

Years passed. Jay and Ellie took car trips with Foxy. They moved to a new house. Foxy got lost and was found, got injured and recuperated. Through illness and loss, obedience and agility classes, the little red-haired dog from the shelter was part of the family. He learned to accept affection from strangers, and enjoyed meeting dogs on his daily walks and in dog parks.

Foxy is now thirteen years old and lives in Napa, California. You can read about his adventures and his opinions on dog parks, cats, and humans in <u>My Leash on Life, Foxy's View of the World from a Foot Off the Ground</u>, or check out his blog, www.myleashonlife.me.

Lenore Hirsch *spent 31 years as a special education teacher and administrator. Dog Foxy started dictating his memoir shortly before Lenore retired. In late 2013, he finally was able to get his teeth around a copy of <u>My Leash on Life, Foxy's View of the World from a Foot Off the Ground</u>.*

Lenore's writing includes a column in the Napa Valley Register, Foxy's blog, *www.myleashonlife.me*, as well as poetry, memoir, food and travel pieces. Lenore and Foxy, now a stately fourteen years old, live in Napa Valley, California. lenore-hirsch@att.net

Found by Felines Friendly and Feral

By Deanna Hotchkin

We'd never sought out cats as both of our sons were allergic and asthmatic. But along came Molly, our sweet little Molly Malone, half-grown and hugely hungry. After she was spayed, we brought her inside for just one night to recover. She's been our inside cat since. Our son began taking allergy shots.

Libby and Sassy were rescued from the side of the road during a volunteer highway clean-up. They live in our heated garage. Trixie was discovered under the hood of our car, and we were able to find a home for her with a heartbroken teen-aged girl whose cat had just died. And most recently, ebony, mitten-toed Emmy found a home with my 89-year-old father after his own 18-year-old cat passed away.

Through the winter, a pretty little white and tiger cat appeared at our door to be fed, scuttling away in a protective crouch the second the door opened, and coming back to crunch only when the door was closed and no humans were in sight. For some unfounded reason, we assumed the cat was a male. In June, he appeared with four kittens, all weaned and ready to eat solid food. The myth of maleness was shattered.

Five more cats to feed and care for seemed like just another chapter in our annual summer cat acquisitions. But this was a daunting prospect, since none of these cats wanted to be touched—just fed. Ferals, I learned.

"Don't name them," my older son warned. But Mama Kitty, Muffie, Rufus, Inky, and Binky were already imprinting their little paw prints on my heart. Each morning when they showed up for breakfast, I'd take my coffee out to the patio and enjoy their antics as they gobbled down the chow and wrestled around with each other, pouncing and practicing their climbing and stealth skills, as I gradually got closer and closer to them—literally and emotionally.

I realized I would need to take action to prevent further litters of kittens. We had made sure each of our other cats were spayed, and believed it was a pet owner's responsibility to prevent unwanted babies. So I began searching for help, and found Carol's Ferals. We borrowed live traps from them, captured the four kittens so they could be neutered, and we discovered they were all males. Muffie is now Murphy. We couldn't get Mama Kitty trapped before she had another litter of kittens, which were still being kept out of sight. When these kittens are weaned, we will renew our friendship again with Carol's Ferals, and hopefully end the new additions to our feral community.

By then, I had done some research on feral cats. None of the reading I'd done was very encouraging about the likelihood of taming these cats, because the kittens were too old to be handled by the time we first saw them. But one day I decided Murphy would probably be okay with being picked up. Painfully untrue. The scratches on my right arm healed fairly quickly, but the bruise from being bitten on my left arm took weeks to fade.

In spite of being wounded by Murphy, I still felt the strongest connection to him. He had his mother's white mitten feet, and that irresistible kitten face you see all the time on cat calendars. So I began my quest of coaxing him ever closer. One day, he touched his nose to my outstretched fingertips. I was ecstatic. At the next feeding time, I held fragrant cat treats on my fingertips, and that little rascal ate from my hand! He was mine!

That frightened, wild creature now trusted me enough to come back to me for as many treats as I would give him. I gave him lots.

Murphy now comes right to me at feeding time and lets me pet him from the top of his head to the tip of his tail as he arches into my touch and purrs. His pleasure cannot possibly equal mine. And now Rufus, an angora tuxedo cat, has also decided to eat from my hand and let me pet him. Patience and persistence have paid huge benefits.

Mama Kitty and Binky will come much closer to me. Mama Kitty closes her eyes as I talk to her, and she has learned that meowing for dinner is okay, but hissing and growling is not. Dinner goes back inside until she can ask for it politely.

Sadly, we lost our precious Inky when he ran into the road before dawn and was hit by a car. My husband and I cried in each other's arms. He is buried near the pine tree in our back yard where the kitties' paths to our patio furrow the grass, and where the sun can warm his grave.

My dad thinks there must be some kind of secret underground for cats that keeps drawing these needy beings to our house. My older son, more pragmatically, thinks they just stay because we feed them. Our son is probably right, but we have no intentions of turning away hungry, homeless cats when we always have food on hand.

Our lives have been enriched by every one of these animals. And the love seems to always stretch enough for one (or
five) more!

Luckily for **Deanna Hotchkin**, *she grew up as the child of two
animal lovers in a small town with no zoning ordinances. Her
family pets included not just a dog and cat, but a pony, two
Bantam chickens, a white rabbit, goldfish, silver-dollar sized
turtles, and salamanders (when they could catch them). Early
on, she learned to respect living things—though she still "re-
spects" snakes from a distance.*

*Cats are Deanna's favorites. Their distinct personalities and
aloof attitudes delight her. Due to their independence masking
their affection, Deanna believes that when a cat chooses you, it
is an honor.*

Changing My World

By Jodi Jarvis-Therrian

"Saving one dog will not change the world, but surely for that one dog, the world will change forever." ~Karen Davison

I cannot say this statement without getting choked up and feeling my heart swell. The life of each animal is so precious. I wish I could save all the poor, discarded animals in shelters and on the streets. To see their sad faces can break our hearts. I think you would have to have a heart of steel to be able to watch the shelter commercials on TV, such as the one that features Sarah McLachlan's In the Arms of an Angel without having your heart strings tugged a little. I change the channel when that particular advertisement comes on. Just because we cannot save them all does not mean we cannot make a difference for one or two. It also doesn't mean we can't help a select few by giving a little time to volunteering, donating or networking. I feel if we all do just a little bit, we can make a difference. I always try to remember what one woman, Ms. Jane Goodall, has accomplished to make a difference. She is my inspiration to always do what I can. I understand we are all busy, and we have to know our limits to stay sane and not take on too many animals. We should not feel bad because we don't have time to help every creature. We have to learn to keep that sacred balance or we can get burned out.

I just cannot fathom throwing a creature away. In this modern world of disposable items, I cannot understand how so many people think it is okay to give up on a life. There is not one person on this earth who does not have an issue or quirk. We are not thrown in prison for having quirks. If that were the case, my husband would have had me locked up years ago, with him following directly behind me.

My heart and soul dog, Odin J, found his way to me from a rescue in Kalamazoo, Michigan approximately 10 years ago. Even though he had a fair share of fears and imperfections, he became the love of my life. I have never loved another being more and we have connected in a way that words cannot properly express. I have tried to help Odin with his issues with continual training that is designed to be fun. He works for his dinner every day and prances around like a puppy, eager to please. All this continuous training has helped him with his issues immensely. He has come a long way, but sadly still has a few fears he has not been able to overcome. I try to keep him safe by knowing his limits and not setting him up for failure. I know if there is a house full of running kids, Odin is safer in a locked room instead of stressing him out and taking a chance that he will panic. I cannot imagine throwing my best friend away just because he has issues. I believe it is like when you say I do in a marriage you mean I do for better or worse. The love and special bond I have received for sticking by my boy for better or worse is priceless. He has become so in tune with me that if I say "uh oh" he comes running to see what I have dropped and picks it up and hands it to me. He has found many a glove on our walks in the woods and has always brought them back to me.

I believe everything happens for a reason. I believe I was given my soul dog, Odin, so I could help others who have dogs with special needs and teach them how to give their dogs the life they deserve. I also believe Odin was given to me so I would become active in educating others on bite prevention. There would be fewer dogs in shelters if education on these topics were more accessible to children and adults alike. As it stands, education on how to both generally approach a dog and how to choose the right dog for your specific household is your personal responsibility. It is important to understand the cute puppy will become a full grown dog with needs of its own. It is not just a toy you can return six months after Christmas because you are bored with it. It is a serious responsibility.

There is nothing better than the gift of rescuing a pet and sticking by it for better or worse. In return you will receive an unconditional love that is so amazing and precious, that surely not only the dog's world but your world will change forever!

Jodi Jarvis-Therrian *is the author of* Furry Philosophy and Memoirs Set in Stone. *She is an artist who has dedicated herself to honoring life with love, in unique ways.*

Jodi is passionate about sharing education with our youth, including the proper way to approach a dog, the "no bite rules" and being a voice for the animals who cannot speak for themselves. www.memorystonesbyjodi.com

A Catastrophic Miracle?

First Place Winner

By Karen Anne Kazyak

I affectionately called it "The Little Shelter Who Could!" Picture this, a little county animal shelter, located in the center of one of the largest, most economically depressed counties in the state of Michigan. With multiple violations from the Department of Agriculture, the shelter was on the cusp of being closed. Four cinderblock walls, an antiquated drainage system, outdated cat cages and dog kennels, poor ventilation, no volunteers, and no medical budget. With only one full-time and one-part time Animal Control Officer to service the entire county, they were expected to pick up strays, investigate neglect and abuse, staff the shelter, receive the public, and care for the animals. Stretched thin, the shelter struggled to meet the basic needs of the animals they served. It began to develop a poor reputation in the community as a place of little to no hope and became known as merely a holding facility for killing.

Very few citizens came looking for their lost pets. Even fewer came to adopt new pets. The dogs and cats who made their way to this animal shelter were doomed. Immediately after their four-day obligatory stray hold, most were euthanized. It was governed by the sheriff's department. This was one of their many responsibilities and frankly, it was apparent this was not one of their priorities, nor area of expertise. Animal health, enrichment and adoption were nonexistent. The negative energy surrounding this shelter repelled the people of its community.

Enter a local animal rescue, asked to help save the shelter from the looming fate of closing. The job at hand was to develop programs aimed at enhancing animal wellbeing and identify ways to inspire the community to reclaim their shelter. The goal was to create a healthy shelter culture; one of hope and infinite possibility. An attainable goal or an impossible one?

The rescue took on the task of providing what Animal Control could not: medical assessment and attention, behavioral evaluations, tender loving care, better nutrition, more creature comforts, exercise, and public exposure which increased owner reclaim and adoption rates. But the rescue was small, and their work was daunting. What was needed was people power! How on earth would this happen with all of the strikes against this facility: its physical location in the middle of nowhere, its poor reputation, and its non-existent community support?

Then it happened! I call some things in life "seemingly catastrophic." What happened next was nothing less than a catastrophic miracle!

It was like any other day at the shelter: busy with cleaning kennels, walking dogs, visiting with cats, and planning projects. A call came in from Animal Control giving us a two-day warning for the intake from a hoarding situation. We were told to gear up for 50 to 80 animals. We worked round-the-clock to prepare for the event: amassing adequate crates, enlisting rescue help, securing veterinary assistance, requesting grooming professionals and stocking up on anticipated supplies. We felt confident in our ability to receive, care for and process these innocent victims. What we did not expect was to receive nearly 400 animals, five times the original number expected.

Texts came flooding over the phone line increasing the number of animals as the day progressed. Our team and the sheriff's department were at the residence in question. A meager 11,000-square-foot house filled with upwards of 380 Shih Tzu's, a few Pomeranians & Yorkshire terriers, two birds, seventeen cats, and a snake. It was a story even the National Enquirer would not have believed. Police cars, cargo vans, and horse trailers converged on the shelter property filled with the most pitiful creatures I had ever seen. The dogs were so filthy and heavily matted that they were almost unrecognizable. Their paw pads were so burned from the urine they were standing in, the dogs could hardly put pressure on them to walk. Their eyes were so infected they could barely see. Many of them had never seen the light of day; never ventured out of the four walls of the filthy home where they were born. Petrified, they clung to one another quivering in corners of the cages they were transported in.

It was a sight etched in memory in my brain. There was no time to comprehend and process what was happening. Once the animals started arriving all we could do was attend to their needs. This was certainly an act that was divinely guided. Our team had never known the likes of such a situation or as I coined it: a Shih-Tzu-ation. Yet we handled it with the grace and expertise of a highly trained disaster relief team. How could that be?

Looking back on it now, it was only by the grace of God that we knew what to do. For those of you who do not believe in Divine Intervention, pay attention. There are miracles happening around us all of the time. You just have to be open to receiving them.

Everything needed was supplied in a timely fashion. Just when the crates in the shelter garage filled up, someone showed up with more in the back of their truck. Just when the volunteers were weary and overwhelmed with the task at hand, car loads of new volunteers arrived, as if they were scheduled for work all along. Just when we were running out of medical supplies, in walked a representative from a veterinary office in a neighboring county with exactly what we needed. Just when the team realized that eight hours had passed without a break, someone sent over carloads of snacks, bottled water and nourishment. If I hadn't lived it myself, I would have never believed it.

I would never wish this kind of catastrophe on anyone, but what I would wish, is some sort of event that renews one's faith in humanity, an event that ignites the belief that goodness does prevail and things do happen for a reason much greater than we can possibly comprehend. These hundreds of dogs and assorted animals of various kinds had a mission greater than you or I could ever know. They metaphorically and literally shined a light on this "shelter in the middle of nowhere."

Before this situation, very few people even knew this shelter existed and even fewer felt moved to be a part of it. Then this seemingly catastrophic event took place and the shelter made national news. Donations came from far and wide.

The Shih-Tzu-Ation became the largest documented hoarding case in the state of Michigan. Community members came out to lend a hand and perhaps volunteer for the first time in their entire lives. This forgotten shelter earned its rightful place on the map and was catapulted into the limelight as an example of what was possible in animal welfare when a community banded together for a worthy cause.

At some core level, everyone wants or needs to be part of something greater than themselves...something that puts things into perspective and helps make sense of this thing we call life. Life will always have its ups and downs. Why? Because it is supposed to. There is magic and wonder in all of it. Trust the process; things in life are unfolding exactly as intended! The flip side of the "seemingly catastrophic," is the "utterly miraculous." Wait for it!

Karen Kazyak *M.A./L.L.P serves both the two-legged and four legged members of our society. A practicing, Humanistic, Clinical Psychologist with extensive non-profit, animal rescue and shelter management experience, she follows her passion spearheading statewide animal welfare initiatives that continue to move Michigan toward a no-kill state of being.*

Rescue is in Karen's DNA. It was passed on to her by her late mother Lauri Kazyak who was a pioneer back in the 60s: a fearless, pro-active, community leader masterful at the art of stray animal management! In Lauri's honor, Karen has dedicated the remainder of her life to the service of the animal kingdom. Whether that takes the form of writing, public speaking, transporting or feet on the ground at a shelter, she has surrendered to her soul calling.

Side by Side

By Marty Kingsbury

It's a hot, sticky, buggy Saturday in July. The sky hangs low and lazy; so Bailey, Zooey, and I decide to go for a swim. We pile into the car. Zooey leaps like the agile, 5-year-old Sato rescue dog that she is, and then Bailey, my sweet, 13-year-old, ninety-seven pound, black lab/German shepherd always-smarter-than-me dog lumbers in with a little help and a lift of the hips.

Oh, to be wet.

Oh, to be cool.

Oh, to be 13 and fishing!

We tumble down the rocks to the water where the world is bright and young. The sun shines with joy. The wind whispers in the treetops. Everywhere there is a soft breeze, cool and embracing. There is a hint of roses in the air.

Zooey swims one lap out to the lily pads and then climbs out to clean her fur and sleep in the sun. Bailey wades the entire spit of shoreline at the foot of the rocks, wagging his tail and leaping on anything that might swim by. I swear I can hear him laugh.

When we wrap up and start to head for home, it happens. Zooey prances up the rocks, but Bailey stumbles.

"You all right, Big Guy?" I ask, climbing down. "You need ten fingers?"

I count to three and try to lift him, but it's more than that. His back legs keep caving out from under him.

I shake the treat tin. He gets up, eats a treat, and we try again, but he can't make it. He looks at me and smiles. He tries to climb, but he hasn't the strength in his hips to get up the rocks. What was once a tiny hill has become Big Sur: a thin cliff of rocks heaving out of the water.

Oh my.

To my left is a morass of underbrush and deep growth. I can't even get through the brush on that side of the beach because it is so thick. To my right is algae, a thick, pea-green soupy algae and lilies that extend deep into the pond. The pond bottom is soft and squishy. Who knows what kind of prehistoric pond creature lurks down there.

I strip off my jacket, my shirt, my jeans, my socks and hide my belly pack with my wallet, my phone, and my car keys. I leave on my underwear, my tee-shirt, and my shoes. I try one last time to coax Bailey up the rocks, and one last time he tries and fails.

I whistle for Zooey and there she is, at the top of the rocks. Ears cocked forward, she awaits her instructions.

"Guard my clothes. I'm going in."

Zooey lies down beside my clothes while I take Bailey by the collar. "Come on, Big Guy. I've fished you out of worse scrapes than this."

Gently I swim beside him, holding his back hips, prodding a little, pulling a little. He swims forward, but the lilies get caught in his toes, and he swims back to the beach at the rocks.

"No, Bailey. Come."

He takes a deep breath and comes. Together we swim through algae and lily pads, my fingers and his toes splurshing through the water jungle, the slime, the greasy, greamy, greepy water.

"It's nice and cool, isn't it, Bailey?"

We swim through underbrush toward the shore. We crawl through the reeds, squeezing through the brambles, slicing and scraping our way onto dry land.

"Zooey!" I call.

Zooey has been waiting on the rocks, right by my clothes, waiting for us to emerge. Bailey lies down to take a little rest.

"Good dog. Zooey, Come! You wait with Bailey, okay?"

Zooey runs down the hill and sits while I rescue my stuff, putting dry clothes over wet. Everything about me squishes and drags. When I turn around, there the two dogs sit, on the trail at the top of the hill, tall and proud, tails to the left, ears up and ready.

"Look at you, you young things!"

Bailey wags his tail. He climbed the hill all by himself. He isn't strong. No, no one would accuse him of being strong, but he is still a warrior, an ancient dog, a mighty lab, all black with his beautiful white tuxedo stripe. Zooey sits beside him, wagging her tail in the dirt. Dust kicks up in a miniscule dust storm of celebration and joy.

"You two are amazing. Come on. Let's go home."

Marty Kingsbury *is a poet, playwright, and novelist living in the Boston area. For the last six years, she has been working with All Sato Rescue, an organization committed to bringing the Puerto Rican street cats and dogs to shelters in the US for adoption. Her novel,* Rescuing Oricito, the Almost True Story of a South American Street Dog, *(Archway Publications) is based, in part, on their rescue of her small golden retriever.*

The Journey
of Four Puppies

By Marty Kingsbury

It's 4:30 on a dark Puerto Rican morning. The morning stars shine through the black-blue sky and, in the darkness, we can hear the waves of the Atlantic crashing onto the shore. Jane and I are waiting for Edi Vasquez of All Sato Rescue to pick us up. She has four puppies for us to bring to Boston. The puppies, she told us, were found by the side of the road. Their mother had been hit by a speeding car, and when a friend found them and brought them to All Sato Rescue, they were cold, wet, and trembling.

Jane and I came to Puerto Rico to see the beach where her little dog, along with her eight puppies, had been found. We wanted to eat dinner along the strip of barbeque pits where mine had been rescued. We have spent six amazing days travelling this little island, driving its highways, city streets, and small roads. We walked the beaches and sought escape from the hot August sun. We saw dogs walking with owners, proud and tall, and we saw other dogs, too many dogs, skinny and scrappy, hiding in the shadows, begging for food, hungry for, yet terrified, of human contact.

And now, this morning, as the sunrise cracks open the horizon of this Puerto Rican night, we become conduits, passengers bringing dogs across the border. We are conductors on an Underground Railroad, legitimate coyotes for puppies, and travelers on American Airlines carrying four 8-week-old, 4-pound puppies to a new life.

They stop us at the check-in counter. One of the soft carrying cases is too big; it will not fit under the seat. Edi tells the woman that she has used this crate before, that it is fine, and that it will fit. The woman shakes her head and says she is sorry, but the puppies cannot go. Roberto, Edi's amazing assistant, speeds back to the house to get a better case. I am tense with worry, but Edi stays calm. The clock ticks by. Flight numbers come and go. The line for security swells. The woman goes onto other things. Finally, Roberto walks through the door, another traveling case in hand.

Edi nods and talks and wends her way through logistics and stewardesses and paperwork and dogs. I don't know how she does it, but she makes it work. We walk through the gates, puppies in hand, and yes, even they have to be searched for hidden explosives. They're adorable. They lick the cheeks of the security officer and she coos right back at them, squeezing their armpits, rubbing their bellies.

And then we are on a plane, four puppies at our feet. They squeak a little, but as we hurtle through space, as the engines hum, as the skies turn blue with another day, they curl up and fall asleep. Jane's puppies find her feet tucked in under their case, and they put their chins on the warm, comforting toes. We can almost hear them snore.

Like magic, two women from Caribbean Connections meet us at Logan Airport in Boston to sweep these young puppies away. We say goodbye to our new best friends and turn to get our luggage.

Jane and I watch the four puppies disappear out the doors of Logan airport. This work, accompanying dogs and puppies on the airplane, is one tiny piece in an intimate network of rescuers. From the Samaritans who coax these dogs into their first crate, to the shelter of All Sato Rescue and the Humane Society of Puerto Rico, to the veterinarians who offer surgery and medicines, to the shelters who put these dogs up for adoption in the United States—together they have rescued literally thousands of dogs from the Puerto Rican streets. It will not take them long to find homes or to know love. Given the chance, I am certain these puppies, like our dogs, will give much, much more then they take.

Marty Kingsbury *is a poet, playwright, and novelist living in the Boston area. For the last six years, she has been working with All Sato Rescue, an organization committed to bringing the Puerto Rican street cats and dogs to shelters in the US for adoption. Her novel,* Rescuing Oricito, the Almost True Story of a South American Street Dog, *(Archway Publications) is based, in part, on their rescue of her small golden retriever.*

First Dogs

By Marty Kingsbury

I remember being born.
I remember before that, too.

My mother's water sloshed
In my ears, sweet and warm.

Her heartbeat gave me rhythm and
Her soft, humming songs filled me with

Hope. Peace. Promise.

But mostly I remember the dogs,
Who came to my dreams.

And licked my soul clean.
They told me my name would be Daniel,

That I would be a teacher,
And friends would come with ease.

They taught me to find comfort in toys I could chew,
To chase a ball with all my heart,

To breathe the wind and know the future,
And to nap whenever possible.

They taught me that tall grass can hold
Wonderful secrets, and that, with a proper roll,

Cool mud will cure depression.

When I was born,
I was ready.

Mamma pushed my carriage around the city block
Humming her songs of hope and promise.

She pointed when I pointed and said, "Yes. Doggy."
But she didn't know what I knew,

That dogs had taken care of my soul.

Marty Kingsbury is a poet, playwright, and novelist living in the Boston area. For the last six years, she has been working with All Sato Rescue, an organization committed to bringing the Puerto Rican street cats and dogs to shelters in the US for adoption. Her novel, Rescuing Oricito, the Almost True Story of a South American Street Dog, (Archway Publications) is based, in part, on their rescue of her small golden retriever.

Seymour's Happenstance

By Karen Koger

"Hi mom, I found a dog."

My 21-year old daughter, Emily, called to give me the news of the little stray that had already found a place in her heart. It wouldn't take me long to realize she didn't find him, but this sweet mongrel found her.

Away at college, living off campus with two roommates in a creaky, white house with beautiful, but worn, hardwood floors throughout the first level, this friendly little guy met Emily at her car out front a few days earlier, tail wagging. A gaunt fellow, it was clear to Emily he had been homeless for quite some time in his young life. With his timid friendliness, she was sure his prior life included human contact, but to what extent she could only wonder and would never know.

"Does he have a name?" I asked, curious about the extent of this new-found relationship between dog and daughter.

"We named him Seymour, because Brendon (one of her roommates) thought he resembles a character from a show we all watch," she chuckled. I could sense the smile on Emily's face as she gave me the details of this little vagrant mutt. Emaciated and flea-infested from life on the streets, she explained his condition as fair with matted, tangled fur. She immediately cared for him with a good flea bath and treatment, trimmed his entangled coat, and started a healthy food plan to add bulk to his lanky frame.

Emily scheduled an appointment with a local veterinarian, whose rates were conducive to a college student's budget, and had him thoroughly checked for any unknown issues. A few minor lesions and infections added a regiment of antibiotics and follow-up appointments to his new routine, otherwise a very healthy and happy mutt. Emily opted out of the DNA tests to pinpoint his breed combination: mutt was a perfect breed.

She planned to have him neutered at the earliest date. The vet estimated Seymour to be around 6-months-old and since no chip was found, the vet recommended Emily have a chip placed if she intended to keep Seymour. Emily told me she had the appointment scheduled to take care of both procedures.

Thrilled to hear Emily wanted to keep Seymour, I began planning a trip to her place. It was time to meet my new little grand-dog!

Emily understood how to care for a dog quite well. Besides working at a doggy daycare while at college, she had loving dogs from the time she was born until just a few months before Seymour entered her life. My first black Labrador, a noble, loyal, and smart companion, Barney, rather stocky and strong, was only two when Emily was born. He took her in as his own, protecting and loving her from the moment I brought her home from the hospital and introduced her to my four-legged, furry 'child.' A special bond between human and canine, Emily loved her Barney who was always gentle with her. When his life slowed and his time had come at 13, Emily was right there to hold him as we said goodbye.

We acquired Darby, a happy and husky 2-year old white Lab, when Emily was about seven and Barney, nine. Darby quickly fit right in with Barney, accepting her place with my alpha dog and she loved Emily just as unconditionally as Barney did. Darby also had a good long life, and we were right by her side, holding her as we bid her farewell through love and tears.

Sammy, another black Labrador, came into our lives when Emily, now around 10, decided Darby needed a new companion after Barney's passing. Darby was six at the time. Emily affectionately dubbed Sammy as our special-needs dog and he never quite grew out of his puppy phase. He had anxiety issues, but was lovable and endearing to us. My heart broke when it was time to make that awful, humane decision for Sammy, 12, blind, and suffering from several afflictions.

My heart broke for Emily who, this time, shared in the decision. She picked Sammy out when he was just a furry butterball, and it was her rightful place for Sammy's sake. Hours passed and tears flowed as we sat with Sammy in a cold, unassuming room at the emergency vet into the late night hours. No expensive operation would give him quality time and we knew that Sammy need not suffer anymore. I cried for our Sammy. I cried for Emily. And I was so proud of the unconditional love my daughter now offered her special doggy. We said our good byes and drove home in a haze of emotional exhaustion.

I was excited to meet my little grand-dog and could hear him bellowing between howl and bark as I got out of my car, parked at the curb in front of the house. Emily tried to hold him on the narrow screened-in porch. Seymour having nothing of it was now standing on the plastic patio table, staring intently, his whole body shaking as he waited for my approach. I laughed. He appeared to have Sammy's anxiety. Seymour accepted me instantly with sloppy kisses covering my neck and chin.

We proceeded inside where Seymour slid all over that dark-brown hardwood floor, his claws tap-tapping, desperately trying to gain traction and landing on his bottom at my feet. He ambled onto my lap and sniffed during a break in his excitement. His long legs looked gangling below his scrawny body covered with a beautiful brown, black, and gray coat. Seymour's oversized tail served as an amusing curiosity that he chased with determination. His face resembled a raccoon, mixed with a terrier. Such a silly looking guy, and I was hooked. I searched inside those big, gorgeous brown eyes in hopes of a glimpse into his deepest thoughts. This little doggy was in for some serious grandma spoiling!

We bonded over the next year as he plumped up with a healthy report from the vet. I was Emily's dog-sitter whenever she needed me to help with Seymour. Twist my arm. Of course, there were times when Seymour tested patience and boundaries.

Most days, Emily took Seymour to work with her at the doggy daycare. He loved going with her, waiting at the door, tail lashing back and forth as he toddled into the car with her. When she worked alone or had other day plans, Seymour was crated and was content in his bed. Emily, now in her own two bedroom, one bath duplex, called me one evening in tears. She discovered loud noises caused severe anxiety for Seymour.

"I don't know if I'm going to be able to keep Seymour," she cried.

"Why?" I didn't want her to give up on him whatever the reason.

Emily explained that she came home to another rather nasty crate mess. The crate and everything in it, including Seymour, had to be washed and scrubbed. I wanted desperately to come and help her clean up, but I resisted. This time, I had to let her trudge through it alone. I knew that she could get through this frustrating moment, but she had to see it for herself. Seymour was her 'baby' and no matter the challenge, her love for this little mutt could sustain the worse mess he may cause, whether intentional chewing, or unintentional mishaps such as this night's chaos.

It was a lousy clean-up night for Emily, but afterwards, when all was fresh, and she dried off the bathed and wet ragamuffin and looked into those beautiful eyes of his, she would see that Seymour gave unconditional love and reciprocation of that love was the only answer.

Seymour was a keeper, and Emily has turned out to be a wonderful parent. Truth is, they were inseparable from the moment they met, each taking good care of and protecting the other. Seymour found his forever home with my beautiful daughter.

Now almost four, Seymour enjoys a very happy life with a great mom and a life-long buddy with Louie, a lovable black Labradoodle who came with his master, Rutledge; Emily's boyfriend of three years and Seymour's other best buddy. Louie and Seymour are content chasing, playing with, and tackling each other throughout the day and snuggling close to each other when it's time to rest.

Seymour was led to Emily because she would give him the love he so needed and deserved. I couldn't be more proud of my daughter. She opened her home and her heart to Seymour. I'm pretty sure that Seymour is the happiest dog ever, and I'm sure there are three Labs who just may have had a hand...er...paw in this happenstance. Seymour definitely found Emily.

Karen Koger *of Douglas, Michigan (her "Mayberry" town by the Lake) is a published poet and writer, with her work appearing in poetry journals, newsletters, and webpages. Her stories have been published in New Voices, an Ivy Tech publication, and her poems published in several editions of Poetry Garden, through Parkside Publications and Raindrop Press.*

In addition to writing, Karen enjoys time with her grand-dogs, dabbles in photography and art, and keeps an active life by the lake with her family. She is currently working on her memoir. Karen can be reached at her newly launched blog – www.writtenperception.wordpress.com

How Many Moms?

By Sharon Langeland

How many moms does it take to raise one tiny orphan kitten—THREE. Yes, looking back on the events of Samson's beginning, I can definitely say it takes three.

It was a beautiful mid-summer morning, a Sunday. The sky was crystal blue, and the air smelled fresh and clean after the humdinger of a storm we had during the night. I was at the barn where I board my horse, concerned about one of the feral cats who was expecting her first litter any day—and you know what they say about storms bringing babies!

I had gone only a few steps into the barn, when I heard a tiny kitten crying in a distressed fury. As my eyes adjusted to the dimness of the interior, I saw the baby squirming frantically in the middle of the cement aisle. As I moved closer, I groaned, seeing the placenta still attached, and the cream colored baby still covered with flecks of blood. "Turn around," I said to myself, "It won't live, and it will just break your heart." I had barely changed direction when my conscience spoke up, *someone who is trying this hard to live deserves a chance at life!* So, I picked the wiggling, screaming baby up after detaching the placenta, and held him close in the warmth of my hands. He was ice cold from the cement floor and I quickly put him under my shirt against my skin. He seemed to give a sigh of relief and fell asleep against the warmth. *Well baby,* I thought, *where is your mama's nest?* I started looking through empty stalls, carrying the now sleeping baby. There, in the dim light of the second stall I came to, lay another baby— dead, still in the birth sac. The mother must have been terrified, and had at least tried to move the baby I was now holding to safety.

Home with me the tiny one went. I made him a bed in an old igloo cooler—the kind that had a removable top. Lined with a soft blanket and a floppy teddy bear for a surrogate cuddle mama, it was almost ready for the baby. Tiny babies must be kept warm, so I filled a Ziploc bag with rice and heated it in the microwave, sticking it under the blanket in the cooler by the teddy bear. I gently set Samson in the nest by the teddy bear, and he rooted snuggling up to the soft fur.

By now, the tyke was hungry and I had no formula or bottles. Where to get them? Would Family Farm & Home be open on a Sunday? To my surprise they were! They even had everything the baby would need to survive, including KMR formula and two different kinds of bottles. I purchased both. When I got home and offered Samson the bottle, he was eager to suck, but the bottle was too big for his tiny mouth. Now what? Ah- ha! An eye dropper was just the right size for now. He quickly sucked down two droppers of the warmed KMR formula. Now he had to go potty. Baby kitties need their bottoms stimulated before they can 'go,' so I moistened a paper towel with warm water, and tried to simulate a mama kitty. It worked, he went potty! This was a strange thing to be happy about.

We settled into a routine of feeding every one and a half hours during the day and every two hours during the night. When the alarm went off for the first 2 a.m. feeding, it felt like a bomb went off. "Don't think about it," I told myself, "just move." Walking in a fog, I prepared the warm formula, tested it, and put the rice bag in the microwave to heat. Samson was screaming by now, and another cat I had rescued the year before (a female named Silky Sue), was growing frantic at the insistent cries. I let her smell him and she tried to take him from me. After the little one had his fill of formula, I set him on the couch by the watchful female. Silky Sue began cleaning him off gently beginning with his milky mouth. She was very thorough, however, she would not clean his butt—she made me do that! I sighed, grateful for the help she was willing to give me. "Okay, Silky," I told her, "I'll feed him and you clean him." So now baby Samson had two mamas. Baby learned quickly about formula and wanted more of it each feeding. That meant the butt cleaning was getting a little messy. My old Min Pin, Magical Mincies Lady, watched the ritual with great interest—her little stub of a tail wagging furiously. She was watching me with what...hope?

Now I've heard it said that dogs don't chase cats because they hate them, but they chase cats hoping a snack pops out. I wondered, since Mincie never had babies, if she would have that maternal instinct. Curious, I held the Samson toward her butt-first and said, "Mincie, lick a baby butt?" She immediately began gently and thoroughly cleaning the tiny kitten, doing a mother's duty. Samson responded in the age-old way—he went potty! From that moment on, Mincie took on the potty duty, always gentle, eager and happy. Baby Samson now had three mamas who began the joyful task of helping him grow and thrive. Although I thought for sure those first two weeks of feeding him every one and a half to two hours would kill me, the other two moms never once complained or shirked their duties to our orphan.

It was amazing watching Samson grow and develop. By ten days, his little eyes were wide open and he was starting to change color. He was creamy white all over at first, but now his ears, nose, tail and legs were starting to get dark. At three weeks he started to get teeth, which had become a full set by four weeks. By now, he was using his teeth to chew the nipples off the bottles he had been using since he was 2-weeks-old. At five weeks, he was eating moist kitten food along with his daytime bottles and I was getting more sleep. He was also starting to use the litter box, thus causing Mincie to lose her job. Finally, by eight weeks, Samson was a happy, healthy puffball of a youngster who turned out to be a Lynx point Siamese with beautiful blue eyes and long puffy fur. Samson made me think of my own mother who passed away a few months before he was born. My mother promised me years ago that she would one day get me a long-haired Siamese. I could just hear her from heaven, "she can have that Siamese, but by golly, she's going to have to work for it!"

In conclusion, how many mamas does it take to raise an orphan kitten? Well, maybe, it really takes four mamas to raise a gift from heaven!

EPILOGUE

Today baby Samson is a healthy 3-year old kitty. The only odd effect of being raised by three mamas is he seems to think he is a dog—my husband's dog! Mama number three, Magical Mincies Lady, passed on in 2013 as a result of diabetes and old age. She, too, was my husband's dog and Samson's mama until the end.

Sharon Langeland *is a retired Senior Living Recreational Therapy Aide, a job she loved. She was raised on a farm in the Coopersville, Michigan area and has always been involved with saving animals. Sharon has been rescuing and placing cats for* *the past 25 years and is a current foster for Harbor Humane of Ottawa County. She loves raising the mommas and babies until a home of their own can be found.*

Sharon is married to Bob and they have two sons, Bob and Eric, who are also involved with cat rescue. They also have two grandsons who are continuing the rescue tradition.

The Fabulous Fin Finds Me

By Kendall Jameson

After my dad's coma lasted six weeks, his doctor, also his colleague, friend, and golf buddy, came to me with the paperwork and a choice. Either he amputated Dad's black and rotting feet or they pulled the plug. My dad had been a larger-than-life wild man: brilliant, with offers of pro-baseball in his youth he turned down to get his PhD.

I signed the papers. Looking back, I wonder at the legality of that; why me and not Mom? Were we trying to protect her? Mom, who'd been my best friend, never forgave me, but at least she dodged my lifelong feeling of guilt.

So, at the age of 35, I worked in a big city with wicked winters at a soulless corporation. My social life became a phone call dragging me back across the state to the small town where my mother lived. I spent every weekend and many nights there. Once she lied about an emergency which caused me to turn down an invitation. When I asked her why, she said, "I'd rather you be unhappy than me." Why didn't I change careers, move home or away? I'm an only child with a house payment.

Only a few weeks later, my vet also presented me with paperwork to sign. My dog's cancer reached the point from where I could no longer avoid my responsibility. Bessie, a collie/German shepherd dog of legendary intelligence, understood every word I spoke to her. For instance, once trotting through a room, she wrinkled up a throw rug. I said, pointing, "Bess, look what you did! Go fix that." Joking, right? She went over and flipped the corner of the rug back with her nose. If you don't believe me, I have witnesses. I could go on, but let's leave it that her loss amplified the misery of that year.

We'd been happy, Mom, Dad, and me. My friends still talk about how much we laughed. Dad's job took him around the world and I went with them until college. Then, it all stopped and I shut down. Nothing got through: not food, not drugs, not booze, not music, not reading, in sum, nothing that formerly defined me. I did get thin, but I don't recommend the method. I fascinated men because I didn't respond emotionally and wasn't around much. And work went better because I didn't care. Can't explain any of that.

On a stormy, cold Saturday morning I ran to the grocery store to pick up some things before I headed out to Mom's. A dirty little boy stepped right in front of me as I sprinted out of the rain. I grabbed his bony little shoulders to keep us both upright.

"Lady," he said, defiantly, looking up into my eyes. "If I go home with this kitty, my dad will kill it."

There in a ragged box crouched a tiny sodden kitten, yelling. Loudly. In fact, my first impression was a pink mouth and lots of tiny teeth. I think I took that box and cat because by that point I just did what I was told. I named him Phineas which means *mouth of brass*.

My vet examined it, pronounced it emaciated and terminally sickly. He counseled I put it down right now. He'd get the paperwork. I said no. No more. So, for months I fed the kitten child-strength chemotherapy which turned him into a little raging beast, not unlike my Mom.

One night, I was unloading a big box filled with those wretched packing peanuts and Phin performed a flying dive into it like a tuxedoed kamikaze. Peanuts erupted everywhere. Then he tore through the house and soared back into the box. Peanuts exploded out and he pursued them all over the linoleum. I laughed so hard I lay helpless on the kitchen floor and he walked up my body to stand on my chest and look into my face, a peanut electro-statically adhering to his head.

Warning: here comes the cliché. Something broke inside me. I swear I heard it. Abruptly, I felt love for that sickly unattractive kitten. From then on, it all got better. Phin's named changed to Fin, for finial, in honor of his trick of balancing, all four feet in a space of two inches, atop his scratching post.

We, Fin and I, took a job across the country, in Phoenix, Arizona. To give you an idea of my devotion to that little cat, once on our way to the vet, I ignorantly drove into a flooded intersection. The construction warning signs didn't even hint the pavement had been removed. I suppose, in the street department's defense, they couldn't anticipate a foot of standing water. Anyway, when my car took a dive and began floating and bobbing toward a canal, I never considered climbing out and leaving Fin in a carrier in the back seat. Fortunately, the rotation of the tires slowly pulled us over to higher ground. I'd always wondered what kind of idiot drowned in a flash flood and now I knew.

The rest of my story is that within months, I found a lovely man. When we first met, Don wasn't sure about cats. Fin did not help by cuddling up to be petted, then rolling over to expose his brilliantly white belly. Touch it at your peril. Don took to carrying Fin around like a football and singing "On Wisconsin."

One night Don came over for dinner. Fin launched himself from the counter, slid across the table dragging the lace tablecloth with him, and came to rest with his chin in Don's plate. Fin froze, then rolled his eyes at me to see if he'd live until morning. I started to laugh. Don said from then on he never harbored illusions of the order of my affections.

Fin loved to ride around in Don's van, balancing on the back seat to look out the window. Other drivers frequently honked and waved. He bounced around on Don's waterbed for hours, chasing the splooching noise. He saw himself in a mirror and believed forever after that there lived a monster at the end of the hall.

I found a decent job, made lifetime friends, volunteered at the animal shelter, and when Mom needed me to give her a place to live while she struggled with dementia, I could be there for her.

Oh, Fin went into remission and lived to be 15 when the leukemia finally got him. Paperwork again. I miss him every day and wish he was here to push his head against my face as he did whenever he could reach it. But, I find each subsequent kitty and dog who adopts me creates laughter and love every day.

A Country in Which You Once Lived

By Sarabeth Loomis

My cat tried to tell me he was dying in idiosyncratic ways. It started with a lack of interest in our usual playtime. Tux never did like to play with store bought cat toys; stuffed mice, lasers, balls…all of the things marketers try to convince us cats love, were completely dull, if not idiotic, to Tux. It was only with a long string of yarn, or occasionally a shoelace, that he came to life. I would drag the string behind me as I cleaned the house, and he would trail me with purpose and more than adequate speed, squatting to wiggle his tail before claiming his kill. Then we would retreat to my room, dancing and rolling until we both eventually settled onto my bed, curling around each other, breathing deeply into a fast sleep, exhausted after our happy game. But as his death approached, he only sat on my bed, twitching his ears.

When Tux came to stay, I did not know I would one day beg for time off work, that I would wipe out my fragile savings, and I would learn about the demands of love all in an attempt to keep him breathing. He spent the first few days lying in the windowsill overlooking the flower garden. It was this behavior that gave me the idea for his full name, The Tuxedo in the Windowsill, conveniently shortened to Tux. He was a large cat, sixteen pounds of pure muscle. He kept his silky black fur exceptionally well kempt, and I remember the vet being surprised that I did not use any kind of coat shiner on him. He had a small white tuft of hair on his chest, a common feature of many black cats, but his presence and large, defined face made him more exotic than any black cat I have ever known.

For the first week, I quietly admired him from a distance, careful not to disturb him as he adjusted to his new home. I rubbed the top of his head when I walked by, but I did not linger. I wondered what he could have been thinking, and I imagined it must have been sad. His previous owner had moved to Texas at a place that did not allow pets. An acquaintance told me if someone did not take him, he would be placed in a box on the side of the road, abandoned. I had no previous intention of getting a pet, but my heart ached for this little kitty. So I took a gamble.

Tux jumped into my backpack before I went to class in the morning three times. The first time I almost didn't notice. I sat staring out the front door watching the snowflakes fall in seventeen directions at once. I was dreading stepping into the cold, like walking through bricks. I was so muffled in my layers and complaints that I almost missed the muffled "mmmmmew." Staring up at me from inside of my unzipped bag were two large yellow eyes, as full as the sun in spring.

Tux became significantly more affectionate during the last few months of his life. At night he began to tenderly bury himself into my chest, wrapping his paws around me. We even went for walks in the woods together, without one of those ridiculous harnesses. We would make our way off the trail and search for little sun spots where we could nap, Tux purring loudly on my chest, eyes squinted upwards like a smile.

I will remember the winter before Tux died as the darkest of my early adulthood. The cold in Upstate New York is a living thing that tangles itself around you, choking you, slowing the exchanges between the red blood cells to a crawl. March was dark. Darkness in the morning. Darkness for dinner. Bare branches against a grey sky. A cosmic loneliness was my shadow.

Walking home from class one day, I slipped on an invisible patch of ice behind my house and hit my head, hard. It was snowing, and I remember feeling nauseous and lacking in strength. An hour passed. I needed to get up, but finding the motivation was difficult. The snow crunched, and to my right, Tux walked past me. He paused, but then kept moving, going toward the house. His cat paws were the only marks in the virgin snow. It was curiosity to follow them that forced me up. They looped around the staircase behind the garden, and led up the stairs to the soft glow of the porch light. That kind of magic can warm five winter months.

Tux stopped eating on the same day that I graduated from college. The sky was overcast, and a light mist was falling. I was running late for the ceremony, as is my habit. Rushing down the stairs while pulling my gown over my head, I saw that Tux had left his food and two treats from the night before untouched. Strange for a cat whose favorite hobbies were eating food and licking himself. This was also the same time that he began hiding. First it was in a closet downstairs he refused to leave. I began to force him out, and then he decided his new place would be underneath the porch. No amount of coaxing could bring him to me. Days passed.

I sat in the waiting room of the vet's office for over an hour, trying to stay awake. An old man sat across from me and stared, but did not attempt conversation. A good neighbor.

"Tux is ready," said the vet from her office. She had a round face that made her emotions difficult to read. She folded her hands on her desk and looked down at Tux, who sat stiffly in his taxi. "Sometimes..." her voice began to lose focus and take on a slower, loftier tone, as if we had entered into a sacred space. "Sometimes, there is no reason for these kinds of things. My opinion is that he is telling you that he is ready to die, and he is trying to force you away from him while he does it. This cat loves you very much."

At 2 a.m. I held Tux in my lap and attempted to force gravy down his throat from a syringe. I sobbed. "Tux," I whispered. "Stay with me." With all of his strength he pushed against me with his hind legs and limped away, to the back of the closet, out of reach. Two hours later I was asleep in my bed, when I felt a dry nose on my cheek. The familiar mmmmew awoke me. Tux curled against me; his purr sounded like a failing window fan. He had not come to sleep with me for two weeks. Life was leaving him, leaving, leaving, leaving...the sensation of holding a dying animal in my arms was a dangerous purity; he was going to leave, there was no stopping him. It was almost peaceful—the collision of sacred and mischief.

I attempted to match my breathing with his. There's an interlude at the bottom of a breath, a little delay between filling up and sighing out that's a perfect stillness you can go into. There's a moment of pause between the heart muscle's beat and pump—an instant of earnest quiet when you're momentarily dead. You can find peace there.

Tux sighed, leaving the room. I followed him down the stairs, to the front door, opening it at just the right moment. Looking through the glass, I watched his figure swagger gently into the dark night. That was the last time I saw him.

The Poet Jack Gilbert wrote that we should think of every lover we've had as a country in which we once lived for a time—remembering the exact details; the cracks of the lips, the veins on the arms like road maps. I don't know if I have ever thought of any of my beaus this way, but after revisiting diary entries from the past year and noting just how many times Tux was mentioned, I realized that his love had been the only thing I could count on for an entire year, other than the ground beneath my feet. Through sun and shadow, he was the little keeper of the house and solitude. Some mornings I'd even turn over and find him lying beside me with his head on the pillow, nose pointed toward the ceiling, like a husband.

I don't know if he really found a place to die away from the house for my sake or not, but my earnest guess is that he did. All I know is that, for the time I had him, I am grateful for having been able to just sit there with someone for whom I didn't have to try to be scintillating or euphorically happy, or even happy at all.

Sarabeth Loomis *was raised in the womb of the Appalachian Mountains in Northeast Georgia, where she learned to dance on tables, sing ballads to the moon, and develop sweet charm. At age 18, she moved to New York for college, where she learned to walk fast and talk faster, how to use the minute hand on a clock, and worship sunshine and warmth. She is now traveling around the world, using words to amplify the magic she finds and share it with anyone and everyone.*

A Chance Encounter

By Vonni Leaver

It was supposed to have been a boating day. A summer girl-friends gathering in Newaygo, Michigan. But the unusual July weather presented a cold misty rain and biting wind that suggested we keep the party inside. By mid-afternoon we stepped out onto the deck to see if the weather had improved, which it hadn't. We noticed how fast the nearby blue spruce trees were growing. Beautiful timekeepers. We discussed their growth and all the fond memories associated with them.

We spotted movement in the tall grass field at the edge of the yard. I thought I saw something orange but I couldn't make it out.

"Is it a squirrel?" I asked.

"Chipmunk, maybe," my sister said. "It's small."

We continued talking, resigned to the crappy weather and turned to go back inside. My friend opened the sliding door and just then I thought I heard a squeak. I turned in the direction of where we saw movement in the field. Some kind of very small animal emerged. It looked just a little bigger than a chipmunk.

"What IS it?" I asked my sister Val. It squeaked again and was taking small wobbly hops towards us.

"Oh my gosh, it's a kitten!" Val said.

Where did it come from? I thought. The field it emerged from was at least 100 yards from the nearest neighbor's barn. The kitten squeaked louder as it tried to hop faster toward us. Val leaned over the deck railing for a closer look. "I think its paw is broken!"

Every time the kitten hopped, it fell forward and planted its little face in the ground.

I ran out to the yard to greet this kitten. What are the chances we would have even seen this injured little soul? The kitten was wet and shaking. Its coat looked to be orange and white, but dulled gray by the earth's elements. It easily fit inside my two hands.

"Well, hi there little kitten," I said softly as I brought it closer to inspect its body. The tiny kitten looked me right in the eyes and squeaked loudly, what it probably thought was a meaningful meow. I felt that it was saying, "Save me, please. I'm worth saving." Which seems what every animal rescuer hears when discovering an animal in distress.

The little kitten's coat was wet and muddy. It had scratches on its face and a cut on the right eye. Its eyes were glazed and milky and the lids appeared heavy. The kitten wasn't putting weight on the left paw, which was bent and definitely looked broken. It then made sense why its little nostrils were packed with wet dirt. We were pretty sure the kitten was female. She didn't have a tail either, which was also very disconcerting.

I wrapped the kitten in a clean dry dishtowel and handed it to Val. Newaygo Veterinary Services was five miles away. I drove while my sister held the little kitten. It purred the loudest motor purr for such a sick little thing. Its nose was very pale, which concerned my sister.

"I'm not sure she's going to make it," Val said. "She doesn't look good."

I gripped the steering wheel tighter. "She's a fighter," I said. "I see it in her face." My thoughts, and heart, raced. *Hang in there kitty, hang in there kitty.*

As I was holding the kitten in the examining room at the vet office, she tilted her chin up and locked her goopy scratched-up eyes on me. She purred so loud! She wanted to live, I could feel it, and she chose me to help her. I strongly felt that, too.

Compassionate Dr. Diane VanderWall estimated that the kitten was 4-weeks-old. When she placed her on the large white scale, her tiny body looked like a speck in the middle of it. The kitten started to shake, then turned to look at me, for reassurance I thought.

"It's okay baby, you're gonna be fine," I said with a hopeful tone. She weighed less than one pound. And as we thought, the news wasn't good.

The kitten was very weak and emaciated. She had hypothermia, pneumonia, and her belly was full of parasites. She also had ear mites, and the vet explained her paw was not broken, but paralyzed due to radial nerve damage near the shoulder. That condition was caused by a separation or pulling of the leg away from the body. This could've happened for a few different reasons that we would never know. The vet discussed her possible challenges of not having a tail. It didn't appear the kitten's tail had been torn off, rather she was born without one. The vet explained that some breeds of cats (such as Manx) were born without tails and functioned just fine, while others had loss of bowel function. If they had no bowel control, they just pooped and peed while they were walking without even realizing it.

Considering the kitten's critical status and the possibility of no bowel control, euthanasia was discussed. I felt a sadness flush my body when I saw the "I'm so sorry" look on the faces of both my sister Val and the vet.

"But do you think she could make it?" I asked. "Can't we at least just give her a chance?"

My sister turned to me and said, "That's what you should name her. Chance." I agreed it was fitting, so that would be her name.

Dr. VanderWall assured me she and her team would do everything in their power to help save her. Like many traumas, the first 24 to 48 hours would be crucial. They bathed her, gave her an antibiotic shot, ointment for the ear mites and medicine for the parasites. Chance was ready for transport. We put some fresh towels in a box, and I gently placed the little kitten inside for the ride home. Whenever I peeked in the box, she looked directly into my eyes. I admired her strength, and knew I was in love with this little fighter.

We already had a cat in our household, and I wasn't certain how my boyfriend would take the news of keeping this little kitten if she survived. But he would understand we at least needed to foster her until she got better. Though by now, I already knew I wanted to keep her. There was a reason she found me. We would teach each other things.

I kept her in our guest room with the door closed and set my alarm for every three hours to feed her because her belly couldn't hold much at a time. She had her baby teeth, so the vet suggested I feed her soft kitten food with warm water. Thank goodness she was a good eater. Eliminating was another thing. She was so tiny, I used a small foil pan liner for her litter box. After every feeding, I would hold a warm washcloth on her bottom and squeeze a little; stimulating a bowel movement like her mother would have done. Because of her paralyzed paw, she had a hard time balancing in the litter box. The poor thing did a few face plants because she did not want my help! Sometimes she would whimper then turn and look in my eyes. *Her belly hurts. Those dang parasites.* Afterwards I would hold her to my chest and she would press her tiny forehead into my chin.

"Please live, little one. I love you," I would repeat to her. Then she would pull away and look me in the eyes again. Just checking, it seemed, or perhaps she was trying to send me a sign of reassurance. Sometimes she would burrow herself into my neck and take a healing nap. I prayed many prayers for her.

Slowly she learned to use the litter box, but it took a few weeks to determine she had the strength to control her bowel movements. Once she got stronger, she got the hang of it. I caught myself clapping when she pooped! And when the first few doses of medicine took effect, she was bright-eyed and very playful. She began exploring and hobbling around the house and in time she met our other cat, 8-year old June (who wasn't too thrilled to meet her!). Now they are good friends and wrestle every morning.

One year later and Chance (nicknamed Chancy Pants) is now healthy and thriving at a whopping six pounds and has a huge, spirited personality. Her paralyzed paw does not bother her and she doesn't even know she is handicapped. Chance inspired me to write a children's book (something I've always dreamed of doing) that teaches children how to overcome adversities and learn how to deal with bullying. I'm so very grateful for this "Chance" encounter. I'm hoping she will be just as much of an inspiration to others as she has been to me.

Vonni Leaver *has a passion for writing and a soft spot for animals. She is currently writing a middle grade children's book series featuring her handicapped kitten, Chancey Pants, that focuses on the challenges of overcoming adversities.*

Vonni lived on the east coast for many years and volunteered at the New Hampshire Humane Society. She currently works as a Director of Sales & Marketing and lives with her musician husband, Jack. They split their time between their home in Grand Haven, Michigan and their cottage in Newaygo, Michigan with their beloved felines- Junebug, Clementine and Chancey Pants.

Going Home

By Ali J. Shaw

The sun is bright in the slats of the blinds as I push myself to get out of bed. I'd be content to sleep another hour, but Henry and I have plans for a hike today. I look down at his plush bed on the floor and expect to see him wag his fluffy black tail. Usually, he wags it so hard, it sounds like a knock at the door. He's still this morning, though. He must be tired, too.

I tiptoe past him. His eyes are open, moving in his head as he watches me walk toward the kitchen. *He'll get up when he hears the food in his bowl*, I think.

But before I make it to the kitchen, Henry screams—a pained squelch that has me running. He's sitting up now, his eyelids fluttering as he nods his head in small movements. He's obviously in less pain when he drops it, but he is trying to lift it to look at me, to plead for my help.

This is not the first time Henry has screamed. Just three months after I adopted him, a lively Lab-chow mix barely a year old, he woke me up screaming into the darkness. It took three emergency vet visits to identify his problem as a back injury—maybe from an incident when he was a puppy or possibly a congenital condition.

"He'll need to be on steroidal pain meds for the rest of his life," the vet said.

"But he's so young. Won't that shorten his life?" I tugged Henry's leash protectively.

"Likely, yes." The vet didn't look me in the eye. Henry nudged my hand. "I wouldn't expect him to live past nine." He closed Henry's chart and reached for the door. "But that's years away yet. Make 'em count."

Unconvinced, I went straight to the bookstore and looked up naturopathic remedies. I started feeding Henry fish oils for anti-inflammation, carrots for tissue regeneration, and glucosamine-chondroitin powder for arthritis prevention. With time, gentle exercise, and supplements, Henry needed the steroids less and less. His flare-ups tapered down to once a week, once a month, and finally only a few times a year.

Now six years later, Henry is happiest on the trails. His flare-ups are rare and not nearly as bad as those early ones— just stiffness quickly remedied by muscle relaxers, massage, and stretches.

What's happening now isn't a normal flare-up, though. He continues to shift uncomfortably.

"Can you walk it out, bud?" I ask, patting my legs to try to coax him up. "Come on, let's get you some food and medicine." He tries to do what I ask, but he can't stand—his back legs have stopped working.

No, it's not time yet! We've done so much to prevent this.

Henry has been my constant. Through friendships coming and going, through love and breakups, he's always greeted me, reminded me to play, to eat, to go outside. Together, we've hiked in the Columbia River Gorge, the Cascades, and the Rockies. He has greeted me every morning with tail wags, and he never fails to bring me a sock at the door when I come home. I've taken countless pictures of his wide smile that seems to say, "Life is grand," something I need to be reminded of from time to time.

Henry came to me when most of the constants in my life had scattered. My college roommates and I had grown apart since they got married. Now they spent their time planning events for married people only. When we did have open group gatherings, they were stiff, especially as my boyfriend of three years challenged each person's intelligence. When they left, he'd ask me, "Why are you friends with them?"

When I called a girls' night and choked out that my boy-friend and I were done, their response was "Well, that's proba-bly good," paired with matter-of-fact nods and an abrupt subject change. This was true, but I wasn't ready to admit it so callously.

That night I decided it was time to get a dog. I'd longed for one since leaving home, but I'd rarely had time between classes and work. Now my graduate course load involved mostly independent study. Time was no longer an issue.

I didn't want just any dog, though. I decided I needed one at least two years old, because I'd never trained a puppy. I wanted a female, because boys always lift their legs. And I couldn't live with a Lab, because you can't keep them out of the water or avoid that wet-dog smell.

Henry's whimper pulls me back to the present. He's stopped screaming, but the pain is still clearly all-consuming. With a friend's help, we make it to the vet. They take him in back to run tests, and I'm left in the bare exam room, my only companion the ticking clock. I watch the second hand lurch around. As I count with it, I notice how it matches its corre-sponding hash mark until it hits :26, and then it's one second off until :49, where it appears to tick twice to get back on track before :00.

I think back on Henry's and my first meeting. When I toured the Oregon Humane Society, I expected to read stats to find a few dogs matching my criteria, play for a bit with each, and easily choose one to take home. The first dog had no interest in me—just in the other dogs passing by the play area. The second barked nonstop in a high pitch, and my ears were ringing by the end of our play session. One jumped so high up her kennel wall, I knew she would easily hurdle my four-foot fence. I sighed, resigned to come back in a week or two.

Then there was Henry. He reached for his kennel door as I walked past and then sat obediently when I held up a treat. But he was a boy, only one year old, and half Lab—matching none of my criteria. I reached through his door to scratch his ears.

"Do you want to visit with him?" the volunteer prodded.

What can it hurt? I thought. *I'll get my dog playtime in and then go home.*

After ten minutes with Henry—playing chase, tugging toys, praising him for sit and stay, shake and come—I couldn't imagine going home without him. I scratched his rump, to which he bobbed his chin up, closed his eyes, and grinned.

Reading the rest of his paperwork, I saw he'd spent most of his life in the shelter. His first family returned him when he was just 4-months-old for being "untrainable." His second owner surrendered Henry because he didn't have enough time for a young dog. Then Henry lived at the shelter nonstop for four months.

"Most people see that he was returned twice and just keep walking," the volunteer said.

I turned toward the sweet boy, his chocolate eyes soft and eager, and I knew he was my family.

As I paid the adoption fee, the cashier's walkie-talkie buzzed and then snicked on. "Henry's going ho-ome! Henry's going ho-ome!" the kennel staff sang in unison.

In the vet's waiting room, I watch the clock's second hand revolve yet again, and realize I haven't been paying attention to the minute hand at all. I have no idea how long we've been here, but it feels like hours.

When the vet returns, she kindly but frankly tells me there's no way to know what to expect. "I'm giving you some heavy-duty muscle relaxers. This could be a permanent condition, but it could also be just a pinched nerve that could return to normal once the pressure comes off of it."

It dawns on me that one naturopathic remedy I haven't used on Henry yet is chiropractic. I just recently heard that animal chiropractors work on everything from horses to ferrets. *I can't believe I didn't think of this before,* I think as I pull out my cell phone, hope already filling my lungs again.

When the chiropractor agrees to see Henry, I realize I'm also terrified. *What if it doesn't work?* I once met a dog in a wheelchair cart, and I wonder if that will be Henry soon.

The chiropractor leads us into a room and takes a minute to bond with Henry, rubbing his ears and offering him a salmon jerky treat.

She makes small talk with me as she seems to massage Henry's back. His eyes lock on me, and he thrusts his chin up comfortably. Within seconds, he's pulled his lips back into a wide grin, and he stands up, walks happily to me, and licks my chin.

I'm stunned until a jolt of equal parts relief and excitement runs through my body. The chiropractor opens the door with a smile and tells us to be gentle.

I nod, singing on the way to the car: "Henry's going ho-ome."

Ali J. Shaw *is a typewriter collector, doughnut eater, and napper. For fun, she writes narrative nonfiction that has been featured in Hippocampus Magazine and at DimeStories.com. For money, she works as an editor and ghostwriter for authors and publishers, and she is the owner of Indigo Editing & Publications. Ali lives in Portland, Oregon, where she hikes with Henry, her more recent rescue dog, Skylar, and her husband, Tim.*

The Howler

Second Place Winner

By Eileen McVety

The first three words of his online profile were all I needed to read to know he belonged with us: Sweet, lovable Finnegan.

In truth, the actual words were Sweet, lovable Isaac, but I find it hard after all this time to refer to our beloved mutt by his rescue-given name. Finnegan said goodbye to Isaac when he said hello to us.

Like a real estate listing, the online profiles of adoptable dogs are written using all kinds of euphemisms. I intentionally avoided dogs described as highly energetic, requiring a patient owner, or needing help being the best dog he can be. Our family wasn't too particular about which breed we wanted. We were simply in search of a pup who would capture our hearts and would get along well with our school-aged daughters and our 2-year-old golden retriever.

Enter sweet, lovable Finnegan. Although his profile described him as a basset hound mix, he looked more like a cross between a beagle and a Vizsla to us. Chestnut-colored hair. Electric green eyes. Floppy ears. White patches on his feet that stretched halfway up his paws like fallen-down sweat socks.

I should pause here to say that as long-time golden retriever owners, we had no experience with hounds. We'd done our homework, of course, and thought to ask whether the puppy we were adopting was a howler. The volunteer we worked with insisted she'd never heard him make a peep. I'm not sure whether her answer would have made any difference as we fell immediately in love with Finnegan. But certainly her claim, coupled with the fact that Finnegan's first few days with us were quiet, led us to conclude that we had lucked into a more serene hound.

And then we heard it.

Since that time, I've heard the sound compared—by family members, neighbors, and passersby—to that of a coyote, a wolf, a fork caught inside a garbage disposal, and a dog whose vocal chords have been severed. I admit that the first time I heard it, I was puzzled. We live in a wooded area and it's not unusual to hear the yelp and screech of various critters, but this was a raw, all-consuming wail that was almost primitive. Imagine my shock when I ventured outside and heard that desperate plea emanating from 25 pounds of fur. As I watched Finnegan pace the lawn, tail erect, I followed his manic gaze until landing upon the source of his angst: a small cottontail rabbit nibbling on a twig. It was to be the first of many howling triggers to follow—cats, deer, and hot-air balloons. In short, anything that moved.

People who live in neighborhoods not all that close to ours insist they can sometimes hear Finnegan from their living rooms. Surprisingly, everyone seems pretty good-natured about it. Some call his howl "distinctive." Others say it makes them laugh. No one has called the police. Yet.

"Is that a howl or a bay?" This scholarly question came from a curious older couple that happened to be walking past the house one evening. I didn't know how to answer them. Although the dictionary notes a distinction between a howl, a bark and a bay, to me, trying to label the sound is a bit like trying to describe physical pain. Is it a sharp pain? A shooting pain? A stabbing pain? *I don't know...it just hurts*! Same thing. I don't know...it's just loud.

I may not know what to call it but I am convinced of its meaning: "I see something moving! I'm excited! I might be nervous. I think I want to sniff this thing. I definitely want to sniff this thing. Do you see it? Look! There it is. It's moving. It's coming near me! No, wait...now it's moving away. Quickly. Come back, moving thing! Let me smell you!"

In the two years since Finnegan joined our family, I can say that his howl, though still jolting at times, has become an endearing part of his personality. Much like his cold snout that insists on making contact with your face first thing in the morning. Or the way he bolts from a sound sleep and cascades down the stairs at the soft unveiling of cellophane-wrapped lunchmeat.

My husband remains convinced that our rescue volunteer knew all along that Finnegan was a howler, but concealed the fact so his adoption would go through. I'm not convinced. I think in all likelihood, Finnegan was never comfortable enough before coming to live with us to make himself heard. He needed to find his forever family in order to express his true nature. And how lucky we are to witness that wonderful nature—sweet, lovable, and audibly joyful.

Eileen McVety credits her two dogs with keeping her active, grounded and ever mindful of the placement of food. A freelance marketing/communications writer, Eileen has written essays and short stories for The Chicago Tribune, Tiny Lights, Philo-

sophical *Mother, Career Woman,* and *The Minetta Review.* Her humor book <u>*Welcome to the Company: or What It's Really Like Working Here*</u>, *was published in 2009, receiving high praise from both Midwest Book Review and the author's mother. Eileen lives in suburban Philadelphia with her husband, two human daughters, and two canine sons.*

A Day in Rescue
I Will Never Forget

By Michele Melvin

I was called by a previous adopter who witnessed an animal being neglected, abused and locked up in a basement most of her life. She called me to ask for help. I called a friend who is a private animal cruelty investigator and we headed to the home in question.

Upon arriving, the home appeared clean from the outside so we assumed it was going to be an over exaggeration of an abuse case. The owners came to the door and we asked to see the dog. The dog in question was a 5-year-old female German shepherd. We explained why we were there, and they brought the dog up from the basement. What I saw next will haunt me furever. The dog walked to the door and wearily down the front steps. Her hair was missing from her ribs down to her feet. I am not sure what I noticed first; the smell of rotten, infected flesh or the sight of her poor soul. I asked the owners her name. They told us her name, which we changed. My next question was why?

As I continued to examine the dog, who seemed to be more excited just to sniff the grass and be outside, Jessica started to explain why she was there, and why she was taking their dog. I listened as I continued to examine the dog who was covered in fleas, infesting her whole body. The fleas were crawling over her eyes and head. You could clearly see her spirit was broken and she was giving up. As the conversation was ending, I stood and asked them if this was okay while I pointed to their dog. They stated they did not think it was that bad and had put her in the basement because she had worms. From that point I knew excuses were going to be made that were not worth listening to. We left with a broken, beat down and barely alive dog who wasn't sure she trusted any human.

The look in her eyes as we drove to the groomer to remove the infestation of fleas and feces was of wondering where she thought she was going. I could only imagine her thoughts as we drove away from her prison. While we waited for the groomer to open up her shop, I ran across the street to get dog treats, bones, water and puppy food to soothe her mind and let her know we were there to help her. As the groomer arrived, we took video of her walking, which she could barely accomplish. We documented what the groomer saw, which was hard to stomach along with the smell this poor soul emanated off her hairless body.

As Stephanie, the groomer, lifted the dog's 37-pound body into the tub you could see the uncertainty in her eyes. We all, Jessica, Stephanie, myself and even Stephanie's son, talked to her sweetly, letting her know it was going to be okay. After her bath and nail trim (her nails were curled around, some touching her paw pads) you could see the urine burns up and down her legs.

She was put back into the car and we drove her to the vet's office. On the way there she continued to eat her snacks and nibble on the puppy food. Free of fleas, I was sure she was feeling better. The vet knew we were on our way with an emergency situation, and when we arrived they welcomed her with open arms. They examined her and found she was malnourished, dehydrated, had overgrown nails, burns from urine and feces, was severely underweight, had hair loss from flea infestation, and desperately needed medication. We also discovered she was a Czech GSD and they are very loyal to their people. Apparently so loyal that she would have died there with them if it would not have been for that one call, that one concerned person, that one animal lover. The vet told us it would be months for her recovery.

From that point on, she would be in a foster home where she was going to get the love, care, safety and patience she deserved right from the very beginning of her life.

After her healing, she went to the vet several times to have her vaccines updated and get her spay scheduled. Some of her nails would have to be surgically cut while she was under anesthesia because they were so long. We were very excited by the vet's good news about this GSD dog. She was gaining weight at healthy speeds! She was walking without limping, where before she had no meat on her pads. She was eating and going potty like a normal dog. She was sleeping on a bed (something she never experienced before) and was engulfed with love by her foster family.

After outpours of love and many donations, we received nearly 100 applications for her, but none of the situations were quite right. She finally had a meeting with someone who would possibly adopt this sweet girl and they got along really well. The next step was adoption and we were so excited!

In the meantime we were informed there were fines and jail time for her abusers and even though no amount seems like enough, it was going to have to do.

We now receive pictures and updates on this once wrecked dog we saved; the dog that had her spirit broken, the dog who had given up.

The dog we now call Bella.

Michele's Rescue *has been doing animal rescue as early as 1997. They are a nonprofit 501c3 organization and the founder of the West Michigan Spay Neuter Clinic in Fruitport, MI as well as the founder of Pet a Pawlooza in Grand Haven. Although spaying and neutering are their main goals in rescue, they also do microchipping, vaccinations, general worming, health checks, grooming, rabies and heart worm testing, and topical parasite control. They are no-kill and take all of their animals back if, for some reason, it was not the right fit.*

They volunteer with other organizations to do transport of animals to other rescues and do home checks for out-of-state shelters. They also investigate animal cruelty cases which involves the police on most occasions.

If you would like more information visit them at michelesrescue.com/ Michele's Rescue on Facebook! If you would like to donate, you can contact them via phone, Facebook, email and website!

Miggy

By HJ Mayes

We lost our Yorkie, Bruiser, in November of 2012, to a devastating and mysterious disease. We watched him deteriorate before our eyes, slowly getting weaker until we made the decision to put him down.

When we came home from the MSU Veterinary Hospital without Bruiser in our arms, the first thing we saw was his red retractable leash hanging on the hook next to the door. He loved to go on his walks before his illness sapped his energy. We couldn't bear to part with that red retractable leash and tucked it away in the coat closet by the front door—out of sight, but never totally out of mind.

We swore we would never have a dog again. Well, I swore we wouldn't. Mark, my husband, didn't say much about my swearing off of animals. I know he missed his little buddy.

In August of 2013, I happened to be perusing the Capital Area Humane Society online, curious about how the dogs there looked (I had never adopted). Just to see.

There were a variety of dogs on the site, their tongues hanging out and ears at attention. The camera caught them in action as though, just before the shot was taken, someone called their name and snapped away, like canine paparazzi.

I typed some criteria in the search engine: Small. Male. Younger than seven. Just to see. Up popped a variety of dogs—including one named McGee.

McGee's photo captured him in extreme close up, showing his jet-black fur and little button eyes peeping from beneath a curly mop on top of his head. He also had a gray muzzle, which made him look wise and brought to mind a butler. He almost seemed to be smiling, with his tongue poking out one side of his mouth. I could imagine that as soon as the picture was taken, he turned his interest to something else entirely.

I texted Mark the picture and told him we should go check out this Humane Society. Just to see.

When we arrived, we were shown to a large room lined with kennels of noisy hounds. Barking and howling with the best of them, from the corner was McGee. I almost didn't notice him because his fur had been shaved since his picture was taken—transforming his coat from curly and thick to short and choppy. I reached into the cage to pet him and felt the cold metal burn into my fingers. He licked and pawed at my hand, his little pom-pom tail wagging—starved for affection and attention. I looked at Mark.

"We have to change that name," he told me, looking at McGee.

A few hours later, we walked out with our dog, McGee. I suggested renaming him Miggy, after Detroit Tigers star Miguel Cabrera, an idea my baseball-crazy husband couldn't argue with one bit. We figured it was close enough to the McGee name he was already used to.

The Humane Society told us he'd been found wandering around Saginaw County hungry and with dirty, matted fur. Animal Control picked him up and thought he might be adoptable. They had no health history, but said he was a Lhasa Apso mix. They only could guess at his age.

We went straight to the pet store for supplies: a new set of bowls, collar, treats, and a retractable leash—this one in blue. We purchased the recommended food and took him to our vet for his first official visit.

He had come home with a hacking, worrisome cough and dry, flaky skin that left dandruff on his dark coat. We dutifully gave him medicine for his cough and eye-dropped his food with special oil that was supposed to make his coat shiny and skin not so dry. It seemed like a lot of work in the beginning.

It was a tentative time, with us getting to know him and him getting to know us. It was like the cautious fellowship of feeling out a new roommate and wondering how it would work out. But it was worth it. He lost the cough and his dry coat became softer and shinier.

He left his first official grooming session prancing at the end of his blue leash, like he was proud of his newly brushed teeth and fresh fluffy fur.

While dealing with the cough and dry skin, we also struggled with house training. Miggy developed a habit of soiling the living room carpet and THEN coming to wake us up to let him out. But he was a smart dog and caught on. Now he waits at the door to be let out in the morning. Setting a regular schedule helped.

I look at him sometimes and wonder about his life before us. I picture him hungry, scared and lonely. I think of him wandering the streets in Saginaw County, hiding, scurrying into the shadows with his tail tucked between his legs at the sound of loud noises. He still flinches at passing cars when we walk him down the road.

Even now, when I lean outside for his chain, he flinches and whines if the metal hits the door frame. Did someone hurt him in his past? Who owned him? Who let him go? Who didn't care?

There is no better feeling than when I arrive home from work, and he's waiting for me, pawing at the sliding glass door. Or if he's not waiting, within seconds of closing the door, I hear the tick, tick, tick of his little toenails on the basement steps. He rounds the corner with his tail wagging furiously and lets out a high-pitched squeak—as though my reappearance after an eight-hour-work shift has made his entire day.

It's funny, because he acts that way whether I'm gone for eight hours, or 20 minutes. The same exuberance—complete with clacky toenails and extreme wagging. Like a dog lottery he wins every day.

The other day, I was cleaning out the closet by the front door when Bruiser's red retractable leash fell to the floor. It had gotten stuck between a box of hat and mittens and an old computer we've been waiting to drop off to salvage. I picked up the leash and thought of Bruiser. There was a point in time I missed him every day, and then there was a point when I didn't think about him nearly as much. There is still a special space in our hearts that Bruiser filled.

We still don't know how old Miggy is or how long he will be with us. But I do know he will spend the rest of his life as a member of our family and one of the best parts of our lives. In a short time, Miggy has carved out his own special place in our hearts, too.

Holly Mayes *has enjoyed writing all her life, but only in recent years began truly exploring and nurturing her passion. Her love of writing began in 5th grade when her short story won the*

Miggy

Young Author's Award at school and she was able to meet a "real-life author." She is a student at Siena Heights University pursuing a B.A. in Professional Communications. She served as student editor and contributor for the 2012 Washington Square Review and has been published in When Women Waken, *(Grief, Fall 2013 Issue). She also enjoys attending workshops, traveling and photography.*

Adding to the Number of Illegal Immigrants

By Stephanie Medlock

There's a certain concussion of the emotions where, in your disorientation, all your good sense is swept aside, and you find yourself behaving in ways that were foreign to you only moments before. I call that *love struck*.

In the months since I became thus infatuated, I've lied, cheated, and stolen, as well as broken several international laws. And I'd do it all again.

It all began innocently enough. My husband and I had been ensconced for a week in our rental house in the lovely Mexican town of San Miguel de Allende.

On the sixth morning of our stay, we opened the door and there was a tiny, four-pound, emaciated puppy, with huge brown eyes and a hurt leg. She clung to the hind quarters of a neighborhood street dog, Walter, whom we had befriended. In his mute dog way, Walter's communication about his companion was perfectly clear: "This kid needs help. You can do it." He shook her off his leg and took his leave.

I picked the puppy up and, to quote Mario Puzo's *The Godfather*, I was "hit by the thunderbolt." One look at her little black face with its funny beige eyebrows and floppy ears, her fleas, her skeletal frame, and her nonetheless absurdly hopeful attitude, and I was a goner. After giving her a plate of chicken, I found a vet who would see her that day and I took her to his office.

"What is her name?" he asked me in Spanish as he gently probed and examined her little body.

"Perdita," I said. "Because she was lost."

"That is good," he smiled. He gave her flea and tick treatment and deworming medication, and we made arrangements for me to return in another week to start her puppy vaccinations.

"We're only here a month," I told him. "I don't know what the regulations are for bringing a dog back to the U.S. I'm afraid it will be very hard."

"Don't worry," he said. "Let's take it one step at a time."

The strange part of this conversation was that until that moment I had not realized my intention to bring the dog home with me to the United States. I had not talked to my husband about this, or really thought further than feeding this puppy and making her more comfortable.

As I left the vet's, however, taking a taxi to a pet store where I bought Perdita a bed, a harness and leash, and the vet's suggested puppy food, I realized this decision had already taken place. Arriving back at our house, I found my husband not the least surprised, and over the next few days, he fell as completely under Perdita's spell as I had. Partly it was her beauty: the shiny black fur (revealed once I gave her a flea bath), the floppy ears, the big brown eyes, and the long legs. But mostly it was her personality. Despite having endured near starvation in her 2.5 months of life, she loved everyone— human and dog—and exuded an air of joyous curiosity.

But problems soon appeared in our goal to bring Perdita back to Indiana. The rules about the size of the carrier we could use in the cabin were vague, but this was minor. More problematic was the fact that she was just too young to be imported legally. She had to be four months old and she would only be three and a half months when we returned home. Related to this was the absolute requirement that she get a rabies shot to be able to enter the U.S. She was really too young to be inoculated, but we had no choice.

I presented these problems to the vet on our next visit, as he prepared to give Perdita a distemper vaccination.

"It's all right," he interrupted, looking at me calmly. "There are the necessary rules of medicine . . . and then there is the rule of law. I will abide by medicine's rules. But there is no risk to the United States if she gets vaccinated closer to her departure."

There certainly was a risk to Perdita. A day after the rabies shot was administered, she began to vomit. Listless and feverish, I wondered in horror if my efforts to bring her home to a better life were going to kill her. It took twenty-four hours of antibiotics and sitting beside her feeding her water from an eye dropper every half hour before the crisis passed.

Our plans to import a small adopted dog soon became the font of neighborhood gossip. The taxi drivers, in particular, commented when they saw me load her into their cars for our various trips to the vet.

"Is the dog sick?" they asked.

"No, I'm just getting her vaccinated so she can come back to the United States with us," I told them.

"So you are going to all this trouble to bring home a Mexican dog?" one of them asked me.

"Well, yes," I said.

"Then why don't you adopt *me*?" he asked. "I would very much like to come to the United States."

That put our infatuation with this little dog in a different light. I was doing the same thing for a dog that many people do when trying to slip into the United States—lying to public officials, violating entry requirements, falsifying documents. Even paying the vet for normal vaccinations took on a more dishonest hue. And the outcome was in no way clear. What if airport officials at either end of the trip told me I could not bring her back with me? What then?

For the next few days I woke in the middle of the night, imagining a U.S. vet denouncing us as we got into O'Hare (if we even got that far) and noting that our little dog was much younger than we reported. But there was no turning back.

By the day we packed to leave for the airport in Mexico City, in addition to our five pieces of luggage, we had a healthy dog, four copies of all her paperwork, two carriers, bags of extra food, and a blanket that smelled of Walter, which I took from the house as her transitional object.

Because our flight left at 7:30 a.m., we'd originally arranged to stay at a nice hotel at the airport the night before. This establishment did not take dogs, however, so I spent several hours online before finding a website listing hotels that accommodated pets in Mexico City. I made a reservation with the first hotel on the list.

Big mistake. I should have realized that paying $39 a night in a major metropolitan area was probably going to provide us with dodgy lodging. I still wasn't prepared for the Hotel Templo Mayor, which sat on a dark street near the Zócalo. The night watchman seemed surprised to see us, but he helped us carry our multiple suitcases upstairs to our third-floor room. The layout of the hotel resembled the prison block from the Netflix series *Orange Is the New Black*. All the rooms had a single window that looked onto an inner courtyard. Our room had bunk beds, a single towel, and no hot water. A dim yellow light hung over the center of the room. But it had tile floors, which were easy to clean up when Perdita left a little memento. We cleaned our teeth with a Coca-Cola purchased from the night watchman and set our alarm for 4:00 a.m.

The taxi ride was short at that hour of the morning so we arrived at Benito Juárez Airport by 5:00 a.m. Once at the airline desk, my fears proved groundless. They had a record of our reservation for the dog and waved us on.

The hang-up occurred at security. When I notified an official I was carrying a dog, he took both my passport and my boarding pass.

"You don't have a stamp that says the airline is allowing you to carry a pet," he said. And we went back to the airline check-in desk. Fortunately, we met an extremely efficient airline representative who assured the security guard that my papers were in order.

Back at security, they had me remove the puppy from her carrier and carry her dangling in my outstretched hands through the metal detector. Then drug enforcement personnel were called in. Wearing plastic gloves, they patted down the puppy to make sure she wasn't hiding drugs in her short dark fur. I'm just glad they didn't do a cavity search.

After this, the flight itself was uneventful. Our final hurdle was U.S. Customs at O'Hare. We were sent to a corner of the arrivals lounge, where we pushed a button to summon a U.S. health official. A woman arrived who checked the dog's vaccination records and congratulated us on rescuing a puppy. We had made it.

This all could have ended like the final scene in the 1967 movie classic *The Graduate*, where, after breaking into his girlfriend's wedding to someone else, Dustin Hoffman's character persuades her to run away with him. The last scene shows the two of them on a bus, she in her wedding dress, and he with an expression that says, "Oh God. What have I done?"

So we, too, might have reconsidered the folly of being love struck once our puppy arrived home, needing nearly as much attention as a human baby. But we haven't. When I look at Perdita at night, curled up against our legs on the bed, with our cat sleeping protectively by her side, I like to think she's living a canine version of the American dream. At the same time, I confess, I send out good luck wishes to the *people* on the other side of our southern border who are trying to do the same.

Stephanie Medlock has been writing continually in a variety of venues and professions since composing and illustrating her first book of fairytales at the age of ten. For many years, she worked at the University of Chicago, where she developed courses for the U of C's Graham School of General Studies, including a series entitled The Writer's Studio, and the nationally known publishing programs.

Her novel, The Lives of Things, has been optioned by Totem Films, for which she also wrote the screenplay. In addition to her book, Stephanie has published short stories and memoirs in magazines such as "Feathered Flounder," "Persimmon Tree," and "Tues/Night," and regularly performs her short pieces at storytelling venues in the Chicago area. She lives with her husband in Indiana and San Miguel de Allende, Mexico.

The Ugliest Rat Dog

By Eleanor Whitney Nelson

"That is the ugliest rat dog I have ever seen. I will not have him in our house."

Frank's words seemed uncharacteristically harsh for someone with a soft spot for dogs. But I understood. My husband was trying to convince himself we should not take in the young stray. Reluctantly, I had to agree. We already had two nice dogs and didn't need a scruffy-looking mongrel. Still, I watched the three wagging tails as the black and white mutt sniffed noses through the chain link fence with Copper, our golden retriever, and Djaga, our labradale.

"He must live somewhere in the neighborhood," Frank said. "He'll go home eventually."

"I don't know. He's been hanging around on and off for a couple of weeks. I think he's a rabbit hunting dog."

"So? The hunter probably lives nearby."

"Could be." Our neighborhood of Lo Curro, on the outskirts of Santiago, Chile, contained clusters of fine homes that were carved into the steep hillside. Many of the country's leaders and prominent businessmen lived there and the president's official residence was one street below ours. Separating these elegant homes with their well-groomed yards, were undeveloped zones filled with tangles of brush and trees, coarse grassland and thickets of blackberry brambles, which often rose well above a man's head while spreading out for hundreds of feet, making them impassable to all but the smallest animals.

Tucked in close to the mansions and throughout the wild areas were simple houses inhabited by men and women who worked as gardeners, chauffeurs and maids, day laborers, and families without employment who foraged off the land. Despite the different social and economic levels, the inhabitants of Lo Curro lived compatibly side-by-side. Frank was probably right; the rabbit hunter might well be our neighbor.

"About the time the dog showed up," I said, "I saw a man with a hunting pack working the blackberry patch along the side of our driveway. There must have been twenty dogs, every size and mix you can imagine."

"Why so many, I wonder?"

"I watched for a few minutes, so I'm an expert." I grinned. "Each type had its own job. Whippets chased the rabbits into the brambles and terriers flushed them out along small, tunnel-like paths. Bigger, heavier dogs waited along the outside edge to bring down the prey. The motliest collection of mutts I've ever seen, but they worked well together. Just in that short time the hunter stuffed three rabbits into his pouch."

"This little rat bum probably spotted you. I can just hear him thinking: There's an easy mark. The heck with this working for a living, I'm gonna take a shot at the good life."

"Do you blame him? A chance at a real home where he doesn't have to fight over scraps? He's covered with nicks and bites."

"I know. You'd adopt the whole pack if you could." Frank laughed before turning serious. "We don't have time for a new dog; we're out of town too much. Look at his teeth. He's hardly more than a puppy. Who'd train him? Let's not complicate things."

"I can't argue with you."

The medium-sized dog with black speckles scattered through his white coat and a pirate patch over his left eye cocked his head as he gazed after Copper and Djaga who had wandered off toward the house. He pawed at the fence and whined, his snaggletooth smile fading.

"Shoo," I said, waving my hand at him. "Go on now. Go home."

"Maybe you should talk to him in Spanish."

I glared at Frank. *"Vaya, vaya!"* I clapped my hands and pointed down the hill.

The rat dog slunk off toward a cluster of eucalyptus trees, circled, scouting out a soft spot, and curled up in the dry leaves. He looked reproachfully at me and tucked his nose under his tail, making me feel like the Wicked Witch. But Frank was right. Our work as exploration geologists took us away for weeks at a time and we would be leaving the dogs in care of the maid. Copper and Djaga were well mannered...but a young stray? Who knew? We didn't need him tearing up the expensive house the company had rented for us, or hurting one of our dogs, or worse, some visitor.

Two more weeks passed and the mongrel was still hanging around, staring hopefully through the fence. Then one day the propane deliveryman arrived with fresh tanks for the kitchen. As he was leaving, I saw the rat dog trot onto the driveway and stop a few feet away from him. For a few moments neither of them moved. Taking a quick glance toward the house, the man scooped up the dog and placed him on the seat next to him. Off they went.

I should have felt relieved, but I didn't. I wanted to run after him, wanted to shout, "You stole my dog." But I didn't. When Frank came home I reported the good news. The dog problem had resolved itself.

Three weeks passed. I had almost forgotten about the rat dog when one morning, as I stood by our bedroom window, I heard a familiar whine. I didn't dare look. I knew the scalawag pirate was grinning up at me. That's it, I thought. Any creature with that much persistence deserves a home. Without second guessing my decision I hurried to the kitchen, filled a bowl with dog food and set it down outside the front door by the black and white mutt. As he gulped the food I studied him. He had filled out since he first appeared at our house seven weeks earlier. No longer was he gangly and ill-proportioned. His sharp puppy teeth were now mature: strong and white, even and clean. As he sat back and licked the remains of dinner off his chops I saw a handsome dog with English pointer in his family tree.

When I reached out to pet his head, he didn't flinch as I had expected. Instead, he dipped his nose and closed his eyes, absorbing the small gesture of affection. I slapped my thigh for him to follow and he walked sedately through the gate into the yard, the picture of dignity and self-assurance. Copper and Djaga greeted him as though he were one of the gang, and the three of them trotted off shoulder to shoulder to shoulder.

Ratso was with us for thirteen years, three in Chile and ten back in the States. This mutt who had once been a stray slipped easily into the good life. He had his own corner of the designated dog couch for a nap after his daily walk, plus he had us—his human servants—to bring him food and toys; best of all, he had acceptance. Always an affectionate fellow, he welcomed newcomers into his pack as earlier members had welcomed him. And during those years, through injuries and a serious illness, he always maintained the same tenacity and robust love of life he demonstrated when he first set out to adopt us.

Eleanor Whitney Nelson is a geologist who, along with her geologist husband, has spent her career working worldwide in mineral exploration. A longtime resident of Arizona, she also devotes her time to writing. Her short stories, memoirs, mysteries and poems have been published in several anthologies, including: Chicken Soup for the Soul (Dog Lover's; Loving Our Dogs), OASIS Journal, The Story Teller and A Way with Murder. Except when she was working in the jungle of Papua, Indonesia and the outback of Australia (where she raised an orphaned wallaby), her family has included one or more rescue dogs.

Growing into Grace

Third Place Winner

By Susan Newhof

Grace is tucked into her nesting box tonight. She has not been well for the past few days, and she is growing weak. Our efforts to diagnose the cause have been unsuccessful. At 5½-years-old, Grace is ancient by commercial chicken standards, but home-raised hens often live happily into double digits. I had hoped for more time with her. When I turned off the light in the coop tonight, I sang Taps to her and our little flock of city layers, as my husband, Paul, and I have done often since we brought them home four years ago.

Grace was purchased with no forethought from a woman I met at a feed store. I was looking for hens to add to our small, newly-assembled flock, and she was eager to part with some of her aging girls. She offered me a 2½-year-old Buff Orpington and a regal Silver Laced Wyandotte of the same age. Both were fat and gorgeous.

"Do you want that one, too?" she said, pointing to the ground near my feet. Just a foot away stood a skinny, nearly-naked chicken I had overlooked in the dim November light. She had no feathers on her back, sides or head. Her wings were bare, except for broken feathers at the tips. And where her lush, bustle-like tail should have been, there was only scraggly plumage sticking straight up.

"What happened to her?" I asked, shocked by this ragged girl who resembled a packaged chicken you'd buy in a grocery store. Was it mites, I wondered, or a vitamin deficiency? The neighbor's dog?

"That's rooster damage," the woman replied. The naked chicken went into the take-home box, too. It cost me just $5 to get her away from her careless owners and the fervent suitors who had plucked her nearly clean.

We called her Grace. "She will grow into her name," I explained to everyone who came to meet our little flock of lovely hens. We dabbed Grace's exposed skin with baby sunscreen on bright afternoons, and in spite of her terrible condition, she settled into life at Chez Poulet and began to lay big nutmeg-colored eggs within a week.

Once a year, chickens renew their feathers by losing and re-growing a good many of them all at once. That's also when, and only when, they fill in any bare spots caused by the loss of feathers earlier. The process is called molting, and it can take several weeks. We hoped that Grace's annual shed was still to come, so she could grow back her feathers before cold weather hit. But it was not to be. When December arrived with a foot of snow, Grace was still nothing but pink skin and broken quills.

I made a tiny cape for her when temperatures continued to drop, and despite the elastic straps that fit neatly around her wings to hold it on, she wriggled out of it. When I draped a square of red fleece across her featherless back one evening as she roosted, she reached over her shoulder, picked it up in her beak and dropped it to the floor. No thank you.

Paul fashioned a dandy heater for the girls and insulated the coop walls and ceiling, which kept its inside temperature above 40F degrees on even the coldest nights. Grace chose to sleep in the relative warmth of a nesting box, cushioned with soft pine shavings, compact and cozy.

It was late spring when I ran my finger lightly across her back and finally felt stubble—the telltale sign of feathers sprouting like toothpicks through her tender skin. In a couple weeks, they began to open, and a month later, Grace was as plush and well-dressed as her flock mates, the color of sunshine on copper.

With those feathers came a new dilemma. Grace started laying eggs with no shells. Normally, the yoke and white are held within a rubbery balloon-like membrane that's covered with a protective, calcium-rich shell. But with no shell, the membrane often tears as the egg is about to be laid. When I would find Grace huddled on the coop floor looking bilious, I knew that sometime in the previous day or two, the contents of an egg would come pouring out of her, leaving the membrane stuck inside, and she would need help to get rid of it. The painless process called for rubbing her vent gently with an oiled, gloved finger, which caused her to push like she was in labor. That usually made the membrane poke out just enough so I could grasp it and slowly tug to remove it. The drama was over in a couple minutes, and Grace headed off to hunt for beetles in the buckwheat and wild violets. This girl was four pounds of tenacity.

Grace has charmed tentative neighbor kids and inspired a book. She feasts on bowls of warm milk and oats on frigid days and naps in the cool shade of our sprawling old arborvitae bushes in the summer. She has had four good years here.

But she has grown frail this fall. She is unusually quiet and inactive, and she is not eating much.

When I moved Grace into a cage in the pantry this morning, I did it, I realized, because it made me feel better to have her close. I wanted to be able to check on her often and see if she had eaten the fish or cottage cheese or grains set out for her. I wanted, simply, to take care of her.

Late in the day, with her food barely touched, I carried her outside to rejoin her flock so, if she wanted, she could scratch alongside them in the fertile earth in search of bugs and earthworms. When it started to rain, the girls headed to the shelter of their coop, but Grace stumbled and seemed perplexed by her surroundings. I carried her the remaining 50 feet.

Chickens love blueberries, and a cupful was thawing on the kitchen counter for their bedtime treat. When I returned with them, Grace was sprawled on the coop floor, wings outstretched as though trying to prop herself upright. I gathered her up and slipped her into her nesting box. It is the same box, first on the left, closest to the door, where she has spent dozens of days and nights since we brought her home to Chez Poulet. She settled in and ate her share of berries, including two stuffed with antibiotics.

I finished singing the familiar Taps and stood quietly in the peaceful darkness for a full minute, listening to the hens breathe. All is well, I whispered again. Safely rest. God is nigh.

This, for me, is the hardest part of raising chickens. It's not chores in mid-January when the outside temperature drops to -3F degrees and the path to the coop is thigh deep in snow. It's not the 90F degree nights in July when we have to get creative to keep the hens cool and prevent dehydration. It is this: saying goodbye to a sweet pet and knowing that Grace does not want to be snuggled in my lap or wrapped in cozy blankets tonight. She does not care to be petted and kissed and comforted. And while she gobbled those blueberries from my hand, that is all she wishes from me now. It is time to leave her alone.

Near as we can tell, darkness feels good to a hen. They let down their guard. They relax and they sleep. I like knowing that. Grace will be warm tonight, and she will feel safe.

This evening Grace reminds me that sometimes the very best thing I can do for a beloved hen whose life is coming to an end is return her to the comfort of her flock and her favorite nesting box, offer a handful of blueberries and leave her with a lullaby.

Note: Grace was humanely euthanized by her veterinarian after she began having seizures.

Susan Newhof *works as a writer and communication consultant for foundations and non-profit organizations and loves working with others to teach, inspire and advocate.*

The Grand Rapids native served as a press officer for the American Red Cross National Headquarters and its president, Elizabeth Dole. She also trained Red Cross communication staff across the country to work on large disaster relief operations and was regularly interviewed by national media. As a member of a Washington, D.C. training firm, she taught presentation and media interview skills to the leadership of Fortune 500 companies, research firms and national associations.

Susan is author of Michigan's Town & Country Inns, *now in its fifth edition. Her first novel,* Spirits & Wine, *is a mystery inspired by the 130-year-old home in Montague, Michigan that she shares with her husband, two adopted dogs, three rescued cats and a small flock of city hens*

The French Feral

By Elizabeth Leis Newman

Minou may have once been a handsome gray and white kitten, but when I met him he did not have markings or colors that would make anyone look twice. Even at his best, he tended to be a little dirty and bedraggled. Parts of an ear were missing and his eyes were often blurry. He didn't like other cats, and avoided most people, although he would sit as a silent sentry on our front porch. That cautious attitude would disappear when he saw me. He would trot over, climb into my lap, purr and drool.

We had recently moved into a house in Baltimore, and were surprised when cats showed up on our back porch. I started putting out food. My boyfriend, Justin, said if we were going to feed the cats, we needed to find a way for them to not have kittens. I found out about a Trap-Neuter-Release program through the Maryland Feline Society. Minou was the first cat we caught, after accidentally ensnaring an angry possum. Along with six other cats in March 2007, Minou was neutered, vaccinated and sent back outside to be a feral cat. We suspected we would never see him again.

A few months after our first TNR outing, Justin, his mother and I were eating chicken on our back porch. I tossed a piece of fat into the yard, and we laughed as Minou slunk across the yard, look at us, picked up the piece, and ran away.

That week, I saw him sitting near the back steps. I came out onto the porch, and he didn't move.

"Here kitty, here Minou," I said softly. He looked at me with disdain.

I went inside and came back out with an open tuna can. He walked slowly toward me and I reached out a hand, using the other hand to dump the food into the bowl. He hissed and ran away.

I kept trying, and soon Minou was letting me pet him. By the fall, if I went outside, Minou would hop in my lap, nuzzling me as he drooled.

I am the type of person who not only becomes attached to people, but to places, time periods, and inanimate objects. I hold onto blankets torn asunder by animals because I believe I can repair them, or to gifts I hate if I like the people who gave them to me. Minou got his name because Justin made me promise not to name any of the outdoor ferals in order to avoid becoming attached to animals that may not be long for this world. For some time, Minou was referred to as "Old Gray and White." I started calling him Minou, though, because that's what my mom would call cats in French, and I defended it as not being a real name, but a nickname. Justin just shook his head.

I began a subtle campaign to let Minou live with us, our other two cats, and foster puppy. While the puppy was agreeable—what puppy isn't?—the two indoor cats, Simon and Eli, were having none of it. They would hiss at Minou through a window, or Eli would launch himself at the back door in an effort to attack. I was certain they'd all become friends in time. Justin and I became engaged in the fall of 2007, and our family unit was built around fuzzy creatures. I wanted Minou to be a part of it.

In a "well kitty visit" to the vet, Minou was diagnosed with Feline Immunodeficiency Virus, which meant he could only live with other cats if they wouldn't fight. After a few attempts, and dealing with Simon scratching Eli badly enough to cause an abscess, we tabled the idea. Winter was coming, and Minou would try to sneak into the warm house. I made some vague entreaties, asking if any friends would be interested in taking a glazed-eyed FIV-infected cat who wasn't particularly affectionate. There were no takers.

There is often no perfect solution in animal rescue. Everyone wants to give an old grizzled cat a second chance where he lives in a mansion, sleeps during the day by a fireplace and at night with a human who adores him. With that an unlikely scenario, I had begun to think of our humble front porch and surrounding haunts as Minou's home. We inherited a sizable shelter from another feral cat advocate, set it on our back porch, filled it with hay, and made sure Minou had fresh wet food and water every day. He became a fixture on our front porch, often sitting by the door and acting like a watch cat. If he went out on the prowl, he would always come running whenever I called. Anytime I felt down, I was cheered by Minou jumping into my lap as I sat on our porch swing. What I lacked in money I made up for in love.

As an outdoor cat, he had a dangerous life. Minou would show up bleeding; he struggled to chew; and he played chicken with cars in the driveway. He was caught in a trap by someone who wanted the neighborhood outdoor cats permanently removed. A neighbor and I freed Minou from the trap in an episode that made us feel like James Bond.

Minou had two and a half good years before it became clear his teeth were causing him a lot of pain. A miracle arrived when our vet offered to donate her services for his dental

Celebrating Animal Rescue

surgery, which would have cost around $1,200 in a traditional setting. The deal was we would drive her and Minou to an animal rescue shelter where they would let her use the equipment in exchange for us making a donation. My husband held the anesthesia mask over Minou as the vet removed most of his teeth. The drooling stopped afterwards, and Minou had a new lease on life. A few months later, he developed an abscess in his neck. Back to the vet, this time for official on-the-books surgery. He came home, and spent the rest of a particularly nasty winter convalescing in one of our bathrooms. Spring came, and he could enjoy the outdoor life again. He had warmed up to some of the friendlier neighbors, and especially to Justin and my mom. I began to plan how we'd build him an enclosure when we moved to Chicago.

In July 2010, I went to pet Minou and found a huge lump. Our beloved vet diagnosed it as a fast-growing osteosarcoma and noted a thyroid problem, a heart murmur, respiratory distress, potential mouth cancer and, of course, the FIV. I asked her what it all meant and she said, gently, "It means he doesn't want to move to Chicago." I was devastated and we took him home for a week to convalesce in our guest bedroom. He began spitting up blood, but still managed to eat tuna. It was clear it was time, but in some ways he was like the Black Knight in *Monty Python* who loses all his limbs and insists on continuing to fight. If Minou could talk, I suspect he may have said, "It's just a flesh wound." Justin and I knew it was the right thing to put Minou down and it was still awful, even though the entire veterinary staff could not have been nicer. I cried for about two days straight, eating ice cream and watching sad movies.

Minou, in some ways, was always a lost cause. While an earlier vet had said he was geriatric, we later learned from our newer vet—she of the dental surgery and sarcoma diagnosis—that he was probably only about six years old, but that having a hard life and maladies had caught up with him faster that anyone would have liked.

Ultimately, I wouldn't change a thing about the three years we had with him. He became feral to survive, but deep down was a cat who wanted love. Once he got a taste of kindness, Minou turned back into who he truly was.

We take risks when we extend ourselves to other humans. There is no telling what manipulation or heartbreak will occur. But animals are fairly straightforward: When you make the effort, it's generally reciprocated.

It is always tempting to overreach with what animals can feel, or to make stories about animal rescue greater than what they are. At the end of the day, this is my version of *Notting Hill*: I was a girl, and Minou was a cat. I asked him to love me, and he did. His body failed him, but I think the vet may have been mistaken about one of the diagnoses: There was nothing wrong with Minou's heart.

Elizabeth Leis Newman is a former newspaper reporter who is now an editor at a business-to-business long-term care magazine. She has been a volunteer with the Guide Dog Foundation for the Blind, Walter Rescue, and Community Cats Maryland. After living in Baltimore for eight years, she now resides in Chicago with her husband, Justin, and four cats: Eli, Simon, Elana and Kitty. She is a graduate of Northwestern University (Go 'Cats!).

The Cat with the Lemon-Lime Eyes

By Rochelle Newman

With the precision of a prima ballerina, the black cat propelled itself onto the only patch of exposed surface. It planted its paws firmly on my father's kitchen table without disturbing his precious piling system, an intricate stacking of junk mail, bills and local newspapers. The stacks were both chaotic and highly ordered. In one, there were several pounds of sweepstakes entry forms that Ed McMahon had sent to my mother, who had died over a decade ago.

"Its junk mail, dad," I said. "You don't need any of it,"

"How do you know what I need?"

Over the years, I made a point of pruning the piles when they grew too unwieldy. Asking for my father's cooperation was futile, so I mostly resorted to grabbing random stacks and sneaking them out to the trash. Eventually, I just gave up. If he wanted to die alone in a house of clutter, who was I to interfere? Though, I could already imagine what the neighbors would say when they found his body.

"That poor old man surrounded by all that paper? The place was a firetrap. I heard his daughter just couldn't be bothered."

Then a friend found a cat she couldn't keep. She had post-ed signs in search of the owner, but no one came forward to claim the black cat with lemon-lime eyes. My father had always liked cats, as did I, though I wasn't sure he could handle one. A cat, it occurred to me, might give him some companionship and us a topic of conversation.

"Give the cat a couple of days," I said. "If you hate it, I'll take her back."

The cat didn't shed. The cat didn't scratch things. The cat could jump up on a kitchen table and leave piles intact. The cat was perfect. And every day, I left work and headed to my father's to see how the two new roommates were getting along. Food, water, a clean litter box; it was all getting done. My father had even cleared away some papers to make room for the cat to sleep on my brother's old bed so she could perch on a pillow and watch the world go by.

Nonetheless, when the call came at midnight I wasn't really surprised. My father insisted that he had not let the cat out. Still, she was gone. It hadn't even been a week and the exper-iment was over. My father wasn't capable of taking care of anyone; not a cat, not himself. When I saw him next, there was nothing left for us to talk about—then two days later the cat came home.

"I heard her meowing," my father said. "I opened the door and there she was. I knew she would come back. That's been my experience with cats."

I continued to drop by each week, not so much to check up on things, but for the first time in my adult life, to spend time with my dad. The lemon-lime cat would entertain us, filling our visits with something other than mom and the past.

Still, the next call I received about the cat caught me off guard. It was from my friend, the one who had set all this in motion. She'd been contacted by a couple who had spotted one of the Found posters, said the cat was theirs. My father insisted it was too late.

"How do we know they're really the owners?" he asked. My explanation that the couple had been out of town and their ownership of the cat could be verified by an implanted ID didn't make things easier.

I placed the cat's carrying case into my car, allowing my father to poke his fingers through the grate of the carrying case one last time.

"She's crying. She's upset. She doesn't want to go."

"I know, dad."

Then I drove off slowly, trying to see through the puddles fogging my eyes.

The next weekend, I decided to find my father a new black cat with lemon-lime eyes. Surely, there were hundreds, if not thousands, of cats that needed a good home. There had to be another one that didn't shed and didn't scratch and knew how to leap onto a table full of clutter without disturbing a thing. The first two pet adoption agencies insisted they would have to interview prospective owners and conduct a home visit. I didn't believe my father would survive such scrutiny, even if he allowed pet adoption inspectors into his home.

There had to be a simpler way to do this—and one that didn't risk disappointing an old man. Surely the ASPCA would let an old man care for an unwanted cat. When an orange tabby, meowed, and a fat, longhaired grey cat nuzzled my finger, I began to question my black-cat-with-lemon-lime-eyes-only bias. Then a black cat that had been dozing on a carpeted cat tower awoke. It stretched and jumped from the tower to the windowsill, unhindered by the extra toes that made its paws look more like hands. "You're coming home with me," I realized, as I looked for someone in charge to make it official.

The ASPCA officer smiled and seemed pleased that the cat with the extra toes would receive a good home.

"He's been here almost six months. So, it's just going to be the two of you?" he asked, handing me a few forms.

"That's right." I'd already decided this time to be prudent and answer all the questions as if this cat was going to be mine. Then, getting swept up in my charade, I added, "Just me—and my husband.'

"Husband?" The officer looked up from his paperwork. "I'm sorry, but we can't release the cat unless everyone in the family is present? He'll have to come by."

All I wanted was a cat for my father. I bit my lip hard. My husband didn't particularly like cats, though it would be fair to describe his affection for cats as greater than for my father. Besides, I knew he'd look askance at my farce and could use that as a pretext to avoid missing any weekend televised football or hockey.

"Did I say husband? I meant father," I said, correcting myself, as if the truth would set the cat free and into my custody.

The ASPCA officer just stared at me.

"You see my dad lives with...I mean, I live with...Never mind."

"We can keep the cat for you until Wednesday," he informed me as I hurried toward the exit. "Just get whomever it is you'll be raising this cat with to come with you."

My last hope was a city run animal shelter. A young female volunteer led me to a large room with floor to ceiling caged cats. I stepped back, peering to see if any black paws or noses were poking out from above. A quick cat scan revealed stray's in every shade of grey, brown, white and red—but nothing in solid black.

"Don't miss the ones on the bottom," she said, noticing that I looked discouraged. Half-heartedly I crouched down for a better view. Then I spotted it—a pair of lemon-lime eyes peering out from the cage on the very bottom row. It was an awkward angle, and I couldn't get a good look at her. But once the door was opened, she sprang from her cage.

"Rub my belly," she seemed to say, as she rolled onto her back, and stretched herself at my feet. She was younger than the perfect cat, more of a kitten than a cat and already pregnant. This would make her less desirable to most people, but it didn't bother me. If I wanted her, I was informed, she would have to be spayed right away, and the pregnancy would be terminated. I'd have to leave the pound empty handed, but this kitty was worth the wait. It would be just a few days.

When I arrived at my father's with the new cat, I had to promise him that no one could take his new cat away. Then he laid out his conditions: "She'll have to be careful, like the other one. And she can't get my papers out of order." Then, as if on cue, the cat leapt onto the kitchen table, toppling a tower of envelopes. I held my breath.

"She'll have to learn not to do that," my father said as he scooped her up in his arms. He held his face close to hers and shot her a stern look. She touched her nose to his. "She kissed me," my father said. "Did you see that?"

I smiled and sighed in relief. She was perfect, too. Then my father and I entered into serious negotiations about which pieces of junk mail should be cleared away. Our new feline friend looked on, swatting the occasional envelope with her paw, as if weighing in with an opinion.

Rochelle Newman is a Los Angeles based writer and advertising executive. She is completing an MFA in Creative Nonfiction at Culver City's Antioch University. An award winning playwright, Ms. Newman wrote and performed the solo show Hipbones and Cool Whip. The play received positive reviews in the LA Times and LA Weekly. Rochelle has written extensively on the subject, with articles appearing in Advertising Age. She has also been published in literary magazines such as Nailed and Lunch Ticket. She is between pets and hopes to adopt someone again soon.

Second Chance

By Karen Phelps

A year after my divorce, my mother spotted an ad in the local paper for a female collie to adopt.

Collies have been a part of my life since the age of twelve. For many years I'd won blue ribbons and trophies showing my collies competitively in the breed ring and obedience. Although I no longer showed, I currently owned two collies: Amber, a sable female 9-years-old, and Serena, a tricolor female 4-years-old. After a difficult divorce, I had the space, and the time, for one more dog.

I called and spoke to the volunteer the dog lived with. She had bathed the dog and untangled her badly matted coat. She told me the collie had been owned by a couple who'd operated a boarding kennel. After selling their property, they left all their dogs behind to be destroyed. This collie was one of several dogs, all different breeds, and the volunteers were desperately searching to find homes. Her story broke my heart, and I arranged to see the dog the next day.

The minute I met her, I knew I'd take her home with me. The collie approached slowly with her tail barely wagging. A 3-year-old tricolor, she was about Amber's size with a full white collar and good conformation. Her demeanor was quiet, as if she didn't know where she was. Her scarred muzzle and lack of confidence spoke of neglect.

They had probably doubled her up with other dogs when space became limited at the boarding kennel. I cried petting her when I felt every rib. How could anyone do this to a dog? It made me so angry.

Although I never rescued a collie before, I didn't hesitate. I put down a deposit and arranged to pick her up a week later after she'd been spayed. It was the Fourth of July, so I named her Julie in honor of the holiday.

A week later Julie came home. Well-behaved and eager to please, she easily fit in. Amber and Serena welcomed her enthusiastically. Julie's visits in the house with the other collies—and alone—went smoothly.

During the day when I was at work, Julie stayed in an anchor fence run next to Serena. But it was Amber and Serena who did most of her training. When Julie barked at something she shouldn't, Amber and Serena lay with paws crossed and told her by their behavior, "No, Julie, we don't bark at that." She quickly caught on, following their example, mimicking their demeanor. I was not surprised. For years I'd watched my older collies train the younger ones.

A year apart in age, Julie and Serena enjoyed playing together. They raced around the yard shoulder-to-shoulder and lay side-by-side chewing their bones. Serena had been fidgety and whiney as a young dog. Now, having Julie as a playmate calmed her. It also forced her to be a role model. In many ways, Julie became the making of Serena. How rewarding it was to see these improvements in Serena's behavior.

Since Julie's arrival I'd been careful to reinforce pack order. Whenever I handed out treats Amber got hers first, then Serena, then Julie. I maintained the same pack order going out the front door or coming back into the house.

Everything went well until one afternoon I handed out chewies on the deck. Within seconds Julie flipped Serena over and held her down by the throat. Serena froze and rolled her eyes at me pleading for help. Even though Serena outweighed Julie by twenty pounds, she did not fight back. Amber, like a canine Dalai Lama, nervously trotted around them as if to say, "No, Julie. We love one another. We don't fight."

I immediately got Julie by the collar and pulled her off Serena. Then I put her in the kennel, alone, to cool her heels for a couple of hours. It was the last time I handed out chewies.

After the chew toy fight, Amber and Serena smothered Julie with kindness. Gradually they taught Julie to share her toys. If Julie growled or snapped at Amber or Serena for any reason, I banished her to the kennel for a couple of hours. She soon realized I wouldn't tolerate growling or snapping at my other dogs.

Julie was not the only one adjusting. Life after my divorce was a challenge for me. I turned to my dogs as I had since childhood. Working full time occupied my thoughts during the day, but I struggled to adjust to this new life without a husband. My scars were not visible like the ones on Julie's muzzle, but they were there nonetheless. Acclimating this new dog to my household took my mind off the emotional turmoil I'd been through during the last couple of years. It gave me something positive to focus on. I saw so much of myself in this mistreated dog. Little by little, as her confidence grew, Julie's sweet personality blossomed. We formed a new pack. Day by day Julie grew more confident and more trusting. Slowly I developed a new life as Julie and I both healed.

There is little in Julie's confident manner that indicates her earlier neglect and mistreatment. Only one thing gives her past away. Whenever I hand out treats, Julie stands several feet behind Amber and Serena as if to say, "I don't want to be too pushy."

Although I rescued Julie, she was the dog who really rescued me. Together we both got a second chance for a new life.

*Obsessed with horses and dogs since childhood, **Karen Phelps** has shown pure-bred collies for several decades in obedience and conformation. Over 40 of her articles appeared in national dog magazines and several collie books. She won three Dog Writer's Association of America awards, the latest for I Loved Them First, a memoir in poems and photographs about the horses and dogs she's shared her life with. She lives deep in the woods of Westchester County, New York with two collies, Rufus and Keri, and Rosebud, her cat.*

How Stella...
Once Fight Dog Bait...
Got Her Groove Back

By Marsha Porter

About twice a week, Animal Control officers bring injured, abused, neglected or diseased animals into the large veterinary hospital Lisa Grivich has worked in for the past 21 years. Like so many of her co-workers, Lisa has adopted some of these animals which would otherwise have been euthanized.

On a hot summer day, a young female pit mix came in with a possible gunshot wound to her right shoulder. Neighbors had complained about dog fighting and a raid led officers to this young dog tied to a pole in a yard with purebred pit bulls.

The fight dogs were taken directly to Animal Control facilities presumably to be euthanized. The injured mix, dubbed Honey Bee by the officer for her caramel colored coat, was delivered to Lisa's hospital for possible treatment.

Honey Bee was limping without a whimper. X-rays revealed not a shot, but a deep, infected dog bite. She was covered with other bite marks in various stages of healing. The bones of her rib cage were prominently outlined as she weighed only 19 of the 30 pounds healthy for her breed and size. A collar, obviously placed on her when she was a young pup, was embedded in the flesh around her neck. It was apparent her former owners had no concern about her outgrowing it; perhaps they never expected her to survive nearly a year in the deplorably violent world in which they'd placed her.

She was also anemic from the fleas and ticks roaming her body. They swarmed the insides of her ears, legs and groin. To make her more comfortable, the fleas and ticks were immediately treated. With antibiotics and two to three weeks of crate rest, her shoulder had a good chance for a full recovery. The promise of a better life was contingent upon someone adopting her.

Everyone at the pet hospital was impressed by Honey Bee's will to live, no one more so than Lisa. It would be a shame if a dog who had come through as much as this one would now be euthanized for lack of a caring owner.

Lisa turned to her husband, Kevin, an artist and mechanic. Over the years, he'd always been a good sport about adopting animals Lisa had fallen in love with at work. This time he was more hesitant. They already had two cats and a dog, and this dog had more issues than any of the others they'd adopted.

Lisa didn't give up. She just asked him to look at Honey Bee when he came to the clinic. He was surprised by how friendly and trusting she was when she greeted him with a gentle tail wag and toothy grin. Moments after meeting the half-starved, scarred dog, he turned to his wife and uttered the words that spelled hope for Honey Bee. "I guess we've got a new dog." They renamed her Stella Mae.

Stella's transition to indoor living was not an easy one. It was obvious she'd never been under a roof and was spooked by the confinement. Since she had to be crated, the couple kept her in a kennel in their bedroom. She quickly adapted to the kennel and sought it as a safe spot.

Household sounds frightened her. If the ceiling fan was on, she'd stare at it quivering. Doors closing, even the pop of the dishwashing tab sealing shut made her jump and shake with fear. She refused to walk through doorways or venture into the hall. Lisa and Kevin had to carry her outside to go to the bathroom.

Stella healed physically and put on much needed weight. Unfortunately, her adjustments to being an inside dog were so subtle that Lisa and Kevin wondered if she'd ever adapt to her new life. They consulted her vet, Dr. Porte, but he counseled them to have patience and everything would work out.

He was right, but the lessons Stella took to heart did not come from the couple; she learned them by watching other dogs. One day she observed Puck, the couple's Rottweiler, playing with his ball in the hallway. As if passing under the doorway and trotting down the hall had never been an issue, Stella just walked out the door and retrieved the ball. After that, Puck and Stella became fast friends, with Stella learning to enjoy more of what life had to offer her in her new home.

Stella travels 141 miles to visit Kevin's mom at Thanksgiving and stays with her when the couple goes on vacation. Kevin's mom refers to Stella as her granddaughter and has been known to make Stella scrambled eggs and rack of lamb during these visits. It was during one such stay that Stella observed Grandma's Doberman, Toby, trotting down the stairs. Though she'd never attempted the stairs at home, she simply followed Toby without hesitation and has shown no fear of stairs since.

Stella showed a fear of water and Lisa and Kevin were worried about what might happen if she fell into their pool.

She'd sit far away from the pool watching as they swam. Kevin decided to acclimate her to the water while showing her the stairs should she fall in and need an out. He'd bring her into the shallow end of the pool, let her paddle, and then lead her to the stairs to make her own exit. This became increasingly more tolerable until she began standing at the pool's edge waiting for Kevin to bring her in. Her new appreciation for water has transferred to walks along the river where she now wades in on her own.

Like Julia Roberts in *Pretty Woman,* Stella deserves to be spoiled. When she's not at Grandma's for special meals, Grandma mails her squeaky toys and special dog cookies. Between the toys from Grandma and those from Lisa and Kevin, Stella's toy basket is now filled to the top. She has a brown leather bomber jacket and a cubic zirconium pendant of her initial. At a robust 33 pounds, she makes quite a picture strutting around in the ensemble.

TV is a shared event with Stella, Lisa, Kevin and their cat Guinness lounging comfortably on the oversized sofa. When it's time to go to sleep, Stella hops on the bed and dives under the covers. She's overcome her fear of enclosed places.

Stella has remained a quiet dog. She rarely barks or whines. A new neighbor didn't even realize she lived next door since he'd never heard her. She gets the attention of her owners by simply standing in the kitchen for food or near the door when she wants to go outside.

The attacks, neglect and abuse of her youth, have not made Stella aggressive. She loves to play with kids and anyone willing to pet her. When she has a medical appointment, she spends the day with Lisa in the office. She's so friendly, that Lisa's fellow veterinary care workers like to pop in for a visit.

The once gentle wag is no longer timid. She confidently wags it wiggling her whole body as she does so.

The Griviches have no regrets about taking Stella home. Her will to live, and later, her eagerness to embrace all the joys life offered her, have been an inspiration to them. They thought they were doing her a favor, but she's returned it tenfold.

Marsha Porter *co-authored the* <u>DVD & Video Guide</u> *from 1986 to 2007. She has taught a film class and written a monthly column. Author of over 200 non-fiction articles, she has also written numerous award winning short stories. A former English teacher, she holds a master's degree in Education, has written a teacher's handbook and credits her writing skills to the nuns who continuously punished her with 500 word essays. She's spent a lifetime in animal rescue and rehabilitation.*

When Pinto Got Paroled

By Joan Potter

The last of the barred doors clanged shut behind me and soon I was standing in front of Sing Sing's huge stone administration building, the prison's main entrance. I was carrying a cardboard carton that held Pinto—a half-grown black-and-white cat—and his cellmate, Missy, an all-black little male named by prisoners confused about his gender.

As I turned to head for my car, I heard the voices of prisoners behind the bars on an upper level. "Goodbye, Pinto," they called.

I was a freelancer for the *New York Times*, and also a volunteer in a Sing Sing writing workshop. The *Times* had assigned me an article about how inmates at two Westchester County prisons not far from my home—women at Bedford Hills and men at Sing Sing—were able to humanize their lives within the confines of a maximum security prison.

It was 1977, six years after the Attica rebellion, when prisons started opening their doors to reporters and volunteers. Restrictions had been loosened, and the media became more interested in what was happening inside the walls. The Bedford Hills women told me about how they altered their drab green uniforms to make them more stylish, how they rubbed Vaseline on red and blue magazine photographs and spread the colors on their lips and eyelids.

Some men at Sing Sing said they made paintings, kept fish tanks in their cells, and had pet cats. The cats had found their way into the prison yard through holes in the old stone walls, and eventually into the cell blocks, where prisoners lured them to their cells by offering tidbits of food. One prisoner mentioned he begged gefilte fish from the Jewish chaplain.

After I finished the article, the paper sent a photographer to Sing Sing, and when my story appeared it was accompanied by a picture of a young prisoner standing in front of the bars of his cell holding a small black-and-white cat. Coincidentally, this prisoner—the owner of two cats—was also in the writing workshop.

A few days later I received a letter from him saying he'd heard on the grapevine that a cat purge was in the works. "They say they will give the cats to the SPCA," he wrote, "but we know they'll put them in burlap bags and toss them into the Hudson."

I got on the phone to the warden. "Are you getting rid of the cats because of my article?" I asked. He said no, the article had nothing to do with it. Cats had begun to overrun the cellblocks, creating a nuisance and unsanitary conditions. They had to go.

After more back-and-forth with the warden over the next few days, he finally said that I could take the prisoner's two cats out of the prison after the next writing workshop.

Toward the end of the session, as the inmates and I sat in a circle of folding chairs discussing that week's readings, the cat-owning prisoner left the room and came back carrying a medium-sized cardboard carton with the top closed. When the workshop ended he placed the box in my arms. The inmates filed down the corridor, back to their cells. I walked the other way, escorted by a guard. When we reached the locked bars at the end of the hallway the guard shouted, "On the gate, two cats, out on parole," and the lock clicked open. One more gate and I was in the lobby and out the door.

I settled the box in my car's passenger seat and drove the twenty minutes to my house, where I tipped the cats out of the carton and led them to their food, water, and litter box. Pinto was wearing a brown leather collar embossed with his name, which must have been created by his owner in the prison crafts shop. I went to bed, and in the morning the cats were nowhere to be seen. After my teenage sons had left for school and my husband went to work, I searched the house, and found the two crouched together behind the television set in the living room.

They gradually relaxed and we began letting them outdoors during the day. But a few months later, when my sons were returning from school, they discovered Missy's body on the street in front of our house. He'd been hit by a car. From then on, when Pinto went outside he seemed more cautious; he spent his time relaxing under a rhododendron bush in front of the house, and we kept a close eye on him.

He grew into a solid, beautiful cat, loving, intelligent, and sweet-natured. But whenever a visiting man with a heavy tread walked into the house, Pinto cowered in fear, no doubt recalling the prison guards who had stomped around the cellblocks.

When Pinto was fifteen, my husband Roy and I retired from our jobs, sold our suburban home, and moved to a log cabin in the Adirondacks. We worried about letting our cat outdoors, fearing he would wander into the woods and disappear— captured by a coyote or becoming hopelessly lost as he tried to make his way back.

But he figured things out and seemed content with his rural existence. In summer, he sat under the pine trees and among the wildflowers, watching chipmunks and red squirrels speed past. On cold winter days he sprawled on the tile hearth in front of the woodstove. He was making a better adjustment than I was.

I often felt lonely and isolated, especially when summer ended and our downstate family and friends stopped visiting. I felt out of place in our small town, where the residents had lived for generations. Sometimes I cried with frustration, railing at my husband about our ill-conceived move.

Pinto was my comfort. When I sat at the kitchen table with my morning coffee, he hopped onto my lap and stayed there until it was time for me to start my day. In the evening, as I lay on the couch reading or watching TV, he curled up on my stomach. In bed, he stretched his warm body next to mine and purred me to sleep.

Two years after our move, Pinto developed a malignant tumor on his side. His vets, Diane and David, removed it and he recovered, but before long another tumor appeared, this time inoperable. He gradually became thinner and weaker. When we let him outdoors, he seemed bewildered. One day he wandered in the wrong direction, and I discovered him crouched on a fallen tree.

From then on when I let him out I followed him as he moved slowly across the grass, stopping now and then to rest in a sunny spot. Then I'd pick him up and carry him back into the house. In the evening I'd carry him to the couch, sit down, and gently lower him onto a soft blanket I'd folded on my lap. Soon even that made him uncomfortable; he chose to spend his days lying on a towel behind the open bathroom door.

Roy and I could see that he was suffering, but we couldn't bring ourselves to choose to end his life. Some mornings as we watched him trudge into the kitchen for a few bites of breakfast, one of us would say, "He seems to look better today," and the other would agree. But of course we were fooling ourselves.

The vets would only lay out our options, leaving us with the final decision. But one day David said, "Pinto has been kind and loving to you for eighteen years. Now you can do something kind for him."

The next day, David and Diane helped Pinto die. Afterward, I wrapped his body in a soft cloth, placed it in a box, and buried it at the top of a small rise that overlooked the cabin. I collected smooth, grey stones from the woods and built a cairn to mark the grave. When our young granddaughters came to visit, they painted bright flowers on the stones, and on the biggest one they printed in brilliant red letters: PINTO.

A few years later we sold our log cabin and moved back to the suburbs. We left behind the chipmunks that ate sunflower seeds from our hands and the hummingbirds that darted past our faces on the way to their feeders. And we left Pinto's decorated grave.

On trips to the Adirondacks to visit friends, I could never bring myself to return to our cabin to see if the new owners had preserved the grave or had dismantled the colorful stones and tossed them into the woods.

Joan Potter is the author or co-author of several nonfiction books, including <u>African American Firsts: Famous, Little-Known, and Unsung Triumphs of Blacks in America,</u> 4th Edition (Kensington, January 2014), and <u>Still Here Thinking of You: A Second Chance With Our Mothers</u> (Big Table, March 2013). Her *articles have been published in numerous magazines and newspapers, and her personal essays have appeared in anthologies and literary journals. She has taught memoir workshops in writing centers, libraries, arts centers, and state prisons.*

She lives in Mount Kisco, New York and can be reached at pintopot@optonline.net.

The Perfect Cat
with Many Imperfections

By Jane Urbanski

Everybody said, "You guys love animals so much. Why don't you get a cat? They're so easy."

So when we saw a longish-haired, blue-eyed, gray and cream beauty available for adoption in a pet store through one of the local humane societies, my husband and I thought, *Why not?* We were passionate supporters of many animal welfare organizations. We gave our money and our time as volunteers, and we had adopted several dogs and rabbits before, but never a cat. We liked cats, but always considered ourselves "dog people." And we had kind of a running joke. I'd see a pretty kitty up for adoption and say, "Let's get him." We both knew it was always in fun for some reason, but that day—two weeks before Christmas in 2006—something made us stop and consider the situation more seriously.

There lay Geoffrey in his litter box, kind of in a trance. That should have been a sign of all the health problems to come, but we didn't know much about cats at that time, and I was taken in by a pretty face. We couldn't think of any good reasons not to adopt this cat. We loved all animals. We could give him a warm and loving home. We would love him unconditionally. And we figured we had the time and resources to give him everything he would need. We filled out the application and a survey that asked us how much we thought a cat would cost. We didn't know, but found out we guessed excessively high. Another omen of more to come. We were approved right away. Our only concern was that he like our three golden retrievers and vice versa, and that the four new housemates would be safe and happy together.

We brought the dogs back to the store, and the employees were shocked. They had never seen four pets so comfortable with each other. Any fears we had were put to rest so we brought Geoffrey home, renamed him Remington and became cat parents for the very first time.

Contrary to what our friends had said, Remi was anything but easy. He immediately started having accidents—wetting everywhere. We didn't know anything about this so we read online about possible physical problems, bladder infections, adversity to change and all the other reasons cats urinate outside their litter boxes. We did everything the experts said— trying different litters, different litter boxes, different places for the litter boxes and having Remi checked for a urinary tract infection. It took a lot of time and money to finally diagnose him with chronic urinary tract disorder. We had just re-carpeted our entire house to the tune of about $10,000, never dreaming that a 12-pound cat could have so many accidents. Much of the carpet would eventually become so soiled we would have to cut it out in pieces. I was just sick about it at first. But if that's what it took, along with various medications, for Remi to be healthy and comfortable, I could live with the eyesores. It was just carpet. It was replaceable; Remi was not.

We lived with this patchwork carpeting for four years before we were confident enough that Remi could be trusted not to destroy new carpeting. It meant we had four litter boxes with pee pads underneath for one cat. But that's OK. It's not Remi's fault. I believe he was just trying to tell us in the beginning that he had a problem and needed our help.

Everybody loves a playful kitten, but we're not like everyone else. As time went on, we learned that Remi had many more health problems. He was never agile like a normal cat. He always walked like a drunken sailor, but we didn't mind. Kittens and cats who dart around all the time and climb the drapes kind of drive us nuts. So we appreciated Remi's slow slinks around the house.

He was also diagnosed with a liver problem, deformed kidneys, digestive issues, separation anxiety, a heart murmur and allergies. Our vet thinks he may have been hit by a car. We do know that we are his third owners. We didn't know this until long after we adopted him, but we learned that he had been returned or picked up as a stray three times. We suspect it was because of his urinary troubles. He probably had accidents and his previous owners threw him out. That makes us so sad. Why didn't they help him? He must have suffered terribly and for such a long time. Why wouldn't they have taken him to a vet and treated his chronic infections? Maybe lack of time. Maybe not enough money. Maybe they didn't know what was wrong, like we didn't at first. I felt so sorry for Remi, but I figured if he hadn't had the series of circumstances he did, then he wouldn't have ended up with us. And for that, I am grateful. There are literally millions of cats in this country that we could have chosen. It would have been a lot easier. A lot cheaper. But it wouldn't have been Remi.

Our family and friends are amazed at everything we have done for Remi, but anyone who has rescued a special-needs pet or ends up with a special pet knows that you don't even think twice about it. Some of the accommodations we make may seem excessive to others, but it's just routine to us. I guess there were times when I would second guess treatment decisions or just want to give up when he was so sick, but we would never quit on him if there was hope. And neither did our vet. When I was running low on hope, she wouldn't let us surrender. She always said Remi was a fighter, and that if he wanted to live, we had to help him. And she was always right. We could never have done it without her.

Our biggest test came two years ago when Remi had a full-blown stroke that left him totally paralyzed and brain-damaged. He had actually gone into the vet for another urinary tract flare-up. After a couple days in the animal hospital, getting fluids and without seeing much improvement, two vets at the clinic recommended an operation to remove his male genitalia. This would have sounded absolutely outrageous and out of the question except that we knew of a couple other male cats who had had this surgery to address chronic urinary and bladder issues with outstanding results.

After learning more and asking a lot of questions, we agreed to the surgery. However, the night before the operation—a Sunday night—we got a call from one of the vets who wasn't Remi's regular doctor, saying that Remi had had some kind of stroke-like episode. At first, we assured her that he was probably fine, that he is always a little "off" because of all his issues and medications. But she insisted this was something much more.

Sure enough, we rushed into the clinic Monday morning as soon as they opened, and Remi was just a limp pile of nothing. His eyes were shifting back and forth horizontally and he was unresponsive. We knew this wasn't good. We had done everything for him, but it looked like we were going to have to say goodbye.

Our primary vet wasn't there that day, and we really wanted and needed her guidance. The vet who was going to perform the operation suggested we still proceed, that maybe he was so sick from the urinary disorder that it could still bring him some relief. We agreed, but also resolved that if he didn't improve quickly—and significantly—we wouldn't let him suffer.

It wasn't quick, but he did improve. Remi spent the next month in the animal hospital, and we went to visit him every day like you would your sick grandmother. Our vet cheered us on and urged us to wait him out. Again, she was right. Remi did improve, but it was painfully slow. First, his eyes stopped shifting back and forth. Then he could lift his head. Then he could raise one front leg. Then he would paddle with both. After many days, he stood on his front legs!

At some point, we thought he might like to go outside during our visits, since we were also taking up an exam room every time. We would spread out a blanket on the grass and sit with him, pleading with him to stand, to take a step, to walk. He looked so pitiful. He had lost almost half his body weight and was down to about six and a half pounds. His beautiful gray and cream coat was dull and matted, and shaved in spots from the IVs. Passersby would stop and say, "Oh, are you saying a final goodbye to your cat?" And we would eagerly reply, "Oh, no. He's recovering from surgery. He's doing much better!" We got some pretty strange looks, but the good doctor had us believing in miracles.

We continued our daily visits, willing Remi to stand, to step, to walk. And one day, he did! He wearily raised his back end and took one step! And fell down. And tried again and took two steps! And fell down. Then it was three, and the next day it was five.

And that's how Remi recovered. The vet said after about four weeks there wasn't anything more they could do, and he would probably recover faster in his own home like people do with their loved ones around. But my husband said he would have to be able to walk, use the litter box and eat on his own before we would be able to manage him at home. Remember we have three big dogs who could so easily trample him.

We took two out of three. Remi had learned to walk again and relearned to use the litter box. But his mouth was still closed up tight like he had lockjaw. We agreed that with as far as he had come, we could feed him with a syringe or baby bottle for the rest of his life.

But it was impossible to get enough nutrition into him, and he was so skinny as it was. Having to dilute his canned and dry food with enough water to get it through a syringe significantly reduced the calorie content. And Remi had so little control of his mouth that half of the gruel that went in seemed to come back out. Just as we were losing hope again, our little fighter rallied, and one day his tiny mouth just seemed to unlock and he went to eating on his own again!

That was two years ago. Remi now has totally recovered from the stroke. His personality is back, and he walks as well as he ever did—like the drunken sailor of old. Plus, he hasn't had any urinary troubles since his operation. His aim isn't that great sometimes, but I was never going to have the confidence to give up those four litter boxes and pee pads anyway. I'd rather have clean carpet, a fresh-smelling house and a happy, healthy cat.

And Remi is a happy cat. People who have rescued animals believe that those pets somehow know how lucky they are. I am one of those believers. I think Remi knows that all the stars aligned for him when he ended up at our house. He quietly lies on our laps or nuzzles our necks as a sign of appreciation. And we're so grateful that we have had a vet who has been so knowledgeable, has gone above and beyond to do research, selected the right treatments and has never given up on him. I am so thankful we were able to afford all the extra care he has required. We didn't know it when we saw him in the pet shop that December day and so easily could have joked about having a pretty kitty and walked on by like we had done a hundred times before. But we were meant to have him.

We didn't rescue him because he had special needs, but that's what has ended up making him so special and endearing us to him. We have spent so much time and energy working with our vet to diagnose his issues, and holding him till he feels better again that we have formed an attachment I don't think we would have ever had with another cat.

Anyone who has rescued a pet who becomes as special to them as Remi has to us, will understand this bond. Maybe they had to see the pet through a serious medical problem. Or maybe the pet helped them through a difficult challenge in life. Regardless of how they forged that bond, adoptive pet parents often say their rescued pet was their perfect pet. That was certainly the case for us. I still hear everybody saying to us, "You should get a cat. You love animals, and cats are so easy."

Well, we got a cat, but it wasn't easy. We sure do love him though. And despite all his health problems, he fits in perfectly with our furry family. For us, he is the "purr-fect" cat.

Jane Urbanski *is a volunteer at Harbor Humane Society, the West Michigan Humane Society, the Missaukee Humane Society and the John Ball Zoo, and a former board member of the*

Harbor Humane Society and the John Ball Zoo Doers volunteer organization.

Her career includes various communications and marketing positions. She is currently a project leader in the Employee Communications department at Steelcase. Jane has a bachelor's degree in Journalism from MSU and a master's degree in Communications from WMU.

Jane lives in Ada with her husband, three dogs, one cat and two rabbits. She can be reached at j.e.urbanski@att.net.

They Bread Him That Way

By Rachel Wolf

May 3, 2001
Dear Diary,

You are brand new to me. I tell you about myself. My name is Lisa. I am a girl and eight years old. I feel lonely becuz I don't have a brother or a sister to hug and play with. I hope I can get a puppy for my birthday. Puppies kiss and cuddle. It would be my friend! I will talk to Mom and Dad AGAIN today and seeeeee if they will pleeeeease let me have a puppy.

Thirty minutes later
Dear Diary,

Mom and Dad are going to let me have a puppy! Yipee!

June 21, 2001
Dear Diary,

I am going to the animal shelter today on my birthday to pick out a puppy. Mom says we are saving a puppy if we buy it from the shelter instead of a pet store. I'm not sure what we're saving it from, but I just know it will be mine to keep forever.

six hours later
Dear Diary,

We brought my puppy Andy home today. Before he could come home with us, he had to have surguree first so he can't make puppies. That makes me sad becuz he is so cute I wish there could be a gazillion more puppies like him. Anyway we took him shopping and bought a little soft bed and dishes for his food and water. He's so soft, but he scratches and bites hard.

morning time
Dear Diary,

Last night I gave Andy my baby blanket to sleep with but he peed on it! Yuck!

night time
Dear Diary,

I fed him his breakfast and dinner and in between I cleaned up a lot of pee-puddles! He runs around a lot. When my friends and me try to cuddle with him he bites our ears.

July
Dear Diary,

We have had Andy six weeks now so that makes him twelve weeks old. He has grown a lot and is looking like a German shepherd. We don't really know what kind of dog he is since he was a stray. He does bite really hard and barks really mean. Dad sez maybe he will be a good guard-dog for us.

August Uncle Bill's Visit
Dear Diary,

Andy is fourteen weeks old now and I don't like playing with him. I put on my raincoat, boots, and my mom's rubber gloves to protect myself from his puppy bites that feel like snake bites. We all have sores where he bites us. Even Mom and Dad are complaining. Uncle Bill came by to visit. Andy bit him on the butt really hard. Then Uncle Bill said something really bad about Andy coming from hell and Mom told him not to swear. I think lots of people are starting not to like Andy. That makes me feel so sad. I thought my puppy would be the most favorite puppy in the hole neighborhood.

Still August - Andy's in trouble day
Dear Diary,

Today Andy is sixteen weeks old. He is so beautiful with very think reddish brown fur, but trying to hug him isn't posibull. I want so much to pet and hug him, but he always snaps at me. Mom took Andy to the vet today to get his vacscenes. Andy was a bad dog. Mom said he growled really mean-like at the vet and tried to bite her. The vet said we need to take Andy to a special vet called an animal beehavyourist to see if we can keep him as a family pet. We all have to go to the apointmint so the beehavyourist can see how we play with Andy.

September
Dear Diary,

I write this with tears. Andy can't be our pet anymore. He can't be anyone's pet. The special vet says Andy has for-ward aggression (I had to ask Mom to help me spell it). He got it because someone bread him that way. I ask the special vet

233

what bread meant (isn't that something you eat?) and why someone would do that. He skipped x-planing the bread part but told me they did it so they can use Andy in dog fights to make money. I didn't understand how people make money from dogs fighting. Mom and Dad said they would x-plane later. Must stop writing on you Diary. Your pages are getting too wet from my tears.

A day I want to forget
Dear Diary,

Because the beehavyourist told my parents that Andy had to be put to sleep forever, my mom is taking him to the vet today. They will give him medicine that will make him do that. But I new this mint he will die like Grandpa Layton did. I try to understand. I really do. But I hurt in my heart and I am angry at the people who made Andy this way! They should be the ones put to sleep forever!!!

September 2001
Dear Diary,

We buried Andy today up north in our family's pet cemetree behind Grandma and Grandpa's house in the woods. He lies next to my cousin Sarah's goldfish, Boo-boo. Grandma and Grandpa's pet beagles are buried there too. They lived to be really old. Everybody else's pets live a long time. Mind didn't. It's not fair! I can't have a brother or a sister and now I can't have a puppy!

February 2002
Dear Diary,

For three months now we have had our beagle, Princess. She was born on the same day I got you Diary, May 3.

They Bread Him That Way

She is two and a half years old, so she is not a puppy, but she is very pretty and sweet and she doesn't pee on anything xcept the grass. We got her from the shelter too. Princess eats our stiks of butter from the dish on the table. She also likes to lick the kleenexes in our tissue boxes. That makes them all wet and sticky. I can take her for a walk on a leash and my friends love to pet her velvety soft ears. She doesn't bite my friends though, like Andy would have. I still think about Andy and feel sad for him. Cruel people made him something he didn't want to be – a mean dog. Dad said they made a mean dog becuz they woodn't know how to treat a good dog since they aren't good themselves.

February Snow Day!
Dear Diary,   No school!
        I played outside today with Princess. She is so funny when she plays in the snow becuz she gets so xcited that she runs around and around in big circles with her big ears flapping up and down then she rubs her face in the snow and then it looks like she has a beard. I look outside my bedroom window as I write this. It is night-time and the snow is falling in giant flakes. I think of Andy and how he never got to play in the snow. Dad sez that if Andy hadn't gone away we probably woodn't have Princess today. Something good came out of something bad. So I hope Andy is in heaven with Grandpa Layton having fun running in the snow and chazing snow-flakes.

*During **Rachel Wolf's** 59 years of life, she has owned seven dogs, one hamster, two guinea pigs, two love birds, one frog, five goldfish, and one pet rock named The Booga-booga Man.*

235

She has taken classes, attended workshops and conferences, and read books on writing. In the end, she learned to write the same way she learned to garden—through trial and error. If it dies, she tossed it and moved on to something else. Rachel loves variety in her garden, just as she does in her writing. She has learned to tell the difference between weeds and flowers she wants to keep. It is the same with words when revising her stories.

Take Me Home!

By Kate O'Neill

A slim, black, velvet paw reached out for my shoulder, and I turned to see a half-grown black kitten, its face pressed against the wire cage. It was trying desperately to get my attention with a little meow and a gentle tug at the top of my shirt.

"Take ME home," the kitten was saying. "I'm the one for you."

I stopped short in front of the black kitten's cage, charmed by its persistence. I had come to the Ingham County Animal Shelter in Mason, Michigan, with my 20-year-old son Kevin, looking for a kitten, or more likely two kittens, to adopt. Still Kevin and I had not seen all the cats in the room. And I had reluctantly agreed with his insistence that we should adopt two cats, realizing that in our busy household of three working adults, two cats could keep each other company. So I knew I had to keep looking.

Just then another kitten caught my eye—an orange tiger from the top of his head, down his back to the tip of his tail, but with snowy white cheeks, chest, and legs.

"Ooh, Kevin, look at this one," I said. "I've always wanted a marmalade cat."

Kevin agreed we should definitely consider this one.

We circled the room full of cages one more time, when I realized I could not possibly invite any cat into our family until I had held it in my arms.

"OK," said the shelter worker. "Which one do you want to hold?"

"The orange and white one over here," I said. "And...We're planning to take two," I explained. Before I could say more, I again felt a gentle pat on my shoulder. I turned to see the little black cat fixing her eyes on me through the wire cage. "And I want to hold this black one," I hastened to add.

In a moment the black kitten was in my arms, nuzzling its head against my neck. Kevin was holding the roly-poly orange and white kitten, who was a little smaller, but plumper than the black one. Kevin and I exchanged cats and quickly decided these were the ones.

There was a good deal of meowing when we had to put them back in their cages while we attended to the adoption paperwork and paid the fees. We would get a partial refund if we came back in a few months with papers showing the cats had been neutered. And we were cautioned not to wait too long, as we had got ourselves a boy (the orange and white one) and a girl (the black one).

Once freed from their cages, the kittens nestled in our arms, as we carried them to my car and deposited them in a blanket-lined carton on the back seat. With Kevin sitting next to the carton to supervise, I drove us all home to East Lansing, fifteen minutes away.

Once home, we unloaded the kittens just inside the door that opens on the driveway. Freed from the box, they started scampering up the steps to the kitchen, the black one in the lead. Halfway up the steps, she turned suddenly on the roly-poly kitten behind her. "Thiiithh," she said with a scowl. "This is *my* house. What are *you* doing here?" Her message was clear. But the smaller kitty hesitated only briefly.

Wanting to avoid a confrontation, Kevin and I each scooped up a kitten and climbed the two flights to my husband's attic study to introduce him to our new family members. The little marmalade cat rubbed around the hassock where Ronald's feet were resting, but the black one jumped up on his lap and climbed up his chest to give him a gentle lick on the cheek. He was obviously charmed by this intimacy.

"What are you going to call them?" Ronald asked. "They're classy cats; they deserve classy names."

"Maybe names from Shakespeare?" I said. I began running through Shakespeare heroines in my mind: Juliet? Rosalind? Portia? I thought back to the black kitten's hissing remark to the smaller kitty, as the two rushed into our house; it reminded me of the sharp-tongued Beatrice in *Much Ado About Nothing*. And the orange and white kitten could be the happy-go-lucky Benedick from the same play.

So they were named. And despite that early confrontation, our kitties, Beatrice and Benedick, soon became fast friends.

They had almost two happy years together, especially in the summers at our Vermont cottage where they often stayed out all night in the woods, like two wayward teenagers. In fact, Beatrice was sometimes gone night and day, but Benedick always showed up by the kitchen door in the morning—until one day, he didn't. We searched through pouring rain for two days before we found him, about a quarter mile from our cottage, in a grassy ditch on the side of the state road. His beautiful fur was drenched from the rain, but with no sign of blood or injury. He must have been killed instantly by a passing car.

Beatrice was not around when we brought Benedick home to lay him to rest in the grave we dug in the yard. Perhaps she was out looking for him on her own—or maybe just roaming her "jungle." But when she got back to the cottage that evening, Ronald showed her Benedick's collar, and Beatrice uttered a wild howl of anguish. We knew then she knew that Benedick was gone forever.

I'm sure she went on missing him for a while, but in time, Beatrice grew comfortable in her role of Only Cat. She reigned as Princess Cat in our household for seventeen years, imperious, yet loving, and an active mouser almost until the end of her life. Then suddenly, she came home from a routine visit to the vet, and flopped over as she tried to get out of her cat carrier. She had had a stroke. We rushed her back to the vet who confirmed it was a stroke, but said she might recover. After a few days it was clear she would not. Our wonderful vet came to our house and explained that she would first give Beatrice a shot to make her sleepy, and then administer the final injection. When the sleep-inducing medication was injected, Beatrice, lying on my lap, stirred slightly. Her eyes closed, but I could still feel the rhythm of her breathing against my stomach. Then the vet gave her the second shot, and moments later I could feel my beloved kitty was gone.

Still, Beatrice and Benedick live forever in my heart.

Kate O'Neill has been a freelance writer and editor most of her working life. For 36 years, until her retirement at the end of 2014, she covered theater and dance for the Lansing State Journal. Her articles have also appeared in Detroit Free Press, Detroit News, Ann Arbor News, as well as Dance Teacher and Dance magazines.

Take Me Home!

Kate lives in East Lansing Michigan, with her two 15-year-old kitties, Ptolemy and Cleopatra (littermates) whom she and her husband Ronald adopted eight years ago after their former owner was no longer able to care for them.

Contact Kate at KOwriter@comcast.net.

Adoption

By D.G. Messinger

We had hoped for a newborn. So when the call came telling us about a two-year-old male we were conflicted, aching to move forward, but nervous about his age. *Adoption.* Three short syllables, carrying painful acknowledgment and joyful hope.

Sitting in hard, molded-plastic chairs, we waited for the final review of our now-dissected life. What seemed an endless process now came to this, the final shot in a tied game. We would meet the prospect face-to-face. My wife fidgeted with forms stuffed in the file jacket on her lap, reviewing again our responses.

"They won't like that we both work full days," she said.

Curious we should need to worry about such a thing. A selection criteria item was that our home be an improvement over his previous home. Ours was comfortable, secure, and had a nice yard, but we both had to work to keep it.

"We'll be fine. Work is just part of the picture. They probably look more at stability, commitment, emotional maturity, and security," I said, reassuring myself more than her.

Our marriage was wonderful, but a singular emptiness remained. We had searched and debated the pros and cons of adoption for months. I was against the idea at first, against risking an awkward union. *Adoption is really a crap shoot, after all, isn't it?* Now we were helpless pawns, willing victims of social science and utopian ideals. Perhaps this would be our time.

"Will we get a health history?" my wife asked, to no one in particular. "We should know everything about any prior diseases. What about family hereditary disease or illness history? We're taking such a chance."

"We'll get all they know. If we're not satisfied, we're not obligated." *Not very reassuring, was it?*

As part of the birth process, you know ancestry and have some reliable clues about future expectations. Appearance, personality, disposition, eye color, tall or short, big nose or short nose—all the physical and emotional traits can be guessed with a degree of accurate expectancy. Of course seeing and holding would give some obvious clues, but wouldn't reveal much about the birth parents or grandparents, the heritage. Were his relatives smart, or the village idiots? Were they aggressive, passive, melancholy? Gentle dispositions? Those traits often carried through generations. We might not know.

And what about the "candidate," a cold name for a prospective bundle of joy? Was he mistreated, abused, now psychologically damaged? We had heard stories of the utter chaos in some birth homes, places where experiences could forever ruin a youngster's psyche. Malnourishment in early life could lead to an endless list of long term health concerns. If you considered everything in adoption, the risks were enormous. And now I was having second thoughts.

My wife interrupted my introspection. "I don't think we have the clinic information. Why do they need that now? Can't we decide on medical providers later?"

That is odd. Why do they need that now? "Are you sure the papers aren't there?" I asked, as she dug and then seized a small envelope.

Our attention was collected as the inner office door opened. Marion Roberts, our main contact through this process, smiled. "A little longer, I'm afraid. He's eating now. A little jumpy this morning. I think he senses it's a big day."

That didn't sound good. "Maybe we shouldn't do this to-day," my wife said. "Maybe come back when he's calmer?" *Are we both afraid to face the moment?*

"No, no it's fine. This is common. New surroundings, and new people handling him," Marion replied, heading off some of our growing panic. "Don't worry, it will work out fine. You won't be disappointed," she assured. "I'll bring him out in a minute, but first we need to finish two small items."

I bet he's calmer than I am right now, because I'm as jumpy as a cat in a dog pound.

Marion continued. "The paperwork is in order and the background checks and references were fine. There was some concern about care arrangements while you work, but your plan is adequate."

"Oh yes, everything is set, right down to the feeding sched-ule, exercise, bathing, just everything!" my wife broke in. "Here's a copy of the plan," she said, forgetting it had been part of our paperwork submissions.

"Another thing," intoned Marion. *Oh, oh, here it comes.* "If you accept the adoption, you must take a class on discipline, training, and developing social skills. Can you do that?"

"Like a parenting class?" my wife asked.

"Yes. It will prepare you for problems that may come up," Marion assured. "There's a lot of stress on young ones at first, and classes are a great way to address issues early. The class meets on Wednesday evenings. Will that fit your schedule?"

Super. Like there aren't enough time demands, now we have to attend classes too. How hard must this be? And are we ever going to meet him?

Marion placed the papers with the class information and sign-up sheet on a clipboard and handed it to me. "Just fill out the top, we'll fill in the rest."

We completed the papers, including the liability releases. Marion took the clipboard and with a quick turn disappeared. Just then, a ruckus of epic proportions erupted behind the door she had pushed through. I resisted the urge to grab my wife and bolt out the front door. When the sounds subsided, the door again opened. Marion held a small bundle, cradled carefully in her arms. We saw light golden hair, a pink nose, and prominent pink ears. His eyes were hazel, with hints of brown.

"What beautiful eyes," my wife exclaimed. "And look, he's smiling!"

When I stepped forward, Marion slid the compact package into my arms.

I was speechless, my wife near tears. He was smaller than we expected, but darn handsome. Looking up from beneath funny bangs, he licked my cheek, and his tail whipped back and forth like a willow in a tornado. My wife got the next tongue bath and he nuzzled us both, first one then the other.

"What's his name," I asked.

"This is Jaws," Marion said. "My, he really likes you! He hasn't acted that friendly with the handlers. You haven't met him before, have you?"

"No," we responded, almost in unison.

"That name. Can we change it?" I asked.

"Yes, but it may take some time before he recognizes a new one. What did you have in mind?"

"Jake!"

D.G. Messinger, *along with his wife Bonnie, have adopted or rescued many cats and dogs during their marriage. Don rediscovered the joy of writing a few years ago and has assembled a collection of short fiction including Beds, Renewal at Horseshoe Bend, The Life Machine, and others. This piece, Adoption, is a partly fictionalized account of the adoption of Jake, a lovable mongrel with personality. When not writing or wading in a river waving a fly rod, Don moonlights as an attorney.*

Love is Love's Gift

By Aaron Hamm

I had been out of college for over a year and looking for work in my field. Countless job applications forced me to examine exactly what I wanted to do before beginning the typical expectations life awaits for us: get a job, lease a car, buy a house, have children.

Deep in my heart I knew I needed to travel the world while I had the opportunity. After researching and eliminating several ideas, the sight was set upon Bangkok, Thailand to teach English. I knew where I would be going. Without a job, I packed my bags and set out on the adventure to teach English in Thailand.

But, as life has a way of placing you where you need to be, I ended up in a small beach town known as Playa Samara in Guanacaste, Costa Rica. Two days before leaving for Thailand, I had a change of heart and switched my plane ticket.

I arrived in Playa Samara on the 13th of October 2013, three days after my arrival in the capital city of San Jose. A google search led me to explore this tiny beach town known for its surfing and its perfect mixture of locals, travelers, and expatriates. Several days after arriving, I was frustrated at not being able to find work. I vividly remember sitting at a local restaurant with a cerveza and thinking to myself, if I am supposed to end up here I will. Looking back I see how important faith in things working out was in guiding this for me.

The next day I returned to that restaurant to eat dinner. Upon paying my bill the woman who owned the restaurant asked me my business about town. It turned out that an international school had opened the year prior and was in need of teachers.

Let's fast forward to mid-April 2013. I had been living in Samara for six months and teaching English to first through third graders. The Easter Holiday called Semana Santa arrived and with it, my Mother came to visit me.

I had been living by myself in a beach front apartment and teaching at Mareas International Homeschool. But despite having the ultimate place to live and way to support myself, something was still missing and I could not put a finger on it. I felt lonely and unbalanced. I gave so much of myself to the children that I never stopped to think what I should give to myself. My Mom and I walked up and down the beach many times talking about life and how I could best help the children to blossom.

The truth is the students I taught were very mentally and emotionally draining, until I reached them with love. In order to teach them properly, I had to find a way to reach each of them at an individual level so they cared about school and looked forward to learning in my class.

Enter the next part of my story—finding a dying stray dog and falling in love with her; and in the process becoming more whole.

Playa Samara has a lot of stray dogs. In fact, within Samara and the towns surrounding, the stray dogs are such a problem that it is common to see emaciated and undernourished dogs roaming around with no home. The dogs found on the beach are no exception, not to mention the ticks that carry a deadly disease called tick fever.

I had been talking with my Mom about adopting one of these dogs, but was worried about how I would bring it home to Michigan. I realized how great I was at coming up with excuses why I shouldn't adopt one, rather than why I should.

I started searching for a dog to adopt and found one. But someone had adopted the dog just the day before me and they even had my same first name! While my Mom and I were floating in the ocean and talking about it, she said to me, "When God thinks you're ready for a dog, one will show up."

As the next week went by we looked at some other dogs, but I still couldn't find one. The last day my Mom was in town was Easter Sunday. For Christians it is a day that symbolizes new life and new beginnings. One hour before she was leaving in a taxi to the airport she mentioned that she had seen a dog lying under a table on the beach. As we were eating breakfast at the beach, I walked out to look at the dog lying in the shade underneath the table. I picked her up and she melted across my lap. At that moment I knew she was the dog for me. I borrowed 10 dollars, rushed to the local store in my bare feet and bought some food, a dish and a collar. The store was out of leashes so I got some rope from a fruit vendor on the street.

I put the water down for her and we said maybe if she drinks for me, she is my dog. She drank. I put the food down. Maybe if she eats, she is my dog. She ate. I tied the twine on her collar. Maybe if she walks, she is my dog. She walked.

As my Mother was rolling away in the taxi back to the airport, I stood there shoeless, with a bag of food, and a piece of twine tied to my new dog.

After taking her to the vet, I learned she was in bad shape. Her ribs were hard against her skin, she was covered in ticks, ears full of mites, with a belly full of worms, hair falling out, and a really bad urinary tract infection. Her energy was so low that she could not walk five stairs off the beach into my apartment; so I carried her.

Once she was healthy enough and had no more worms, I began to bring her into my classroom every day. She taught the students about having empathy and how to show love to an animal. They would run in every morning asking about her, petting her, and reading stories to her. She even had a favorite book!

Over time, I began to come into my own as a teacher and the students' behavior began to drastically improve and calm down. They loved to read to her. She went on field trips with us and was a constant source of calming, motivational energy for the classroom.

My life began to change, too. I was busy giving so much love to her I felt myself begin to change as a person. The focus was no longer on me, but on giving love to this dog and making her healthy. Every day I would check her for ticks and walk her on the beach. I would sit next to her and watch her eat and drink. As she began to come to life, she loved to chase wildlife and play with the other dogs on the beach.

She went everywhere with me whenever I left the house. She sat in my lap during dinner at restaurants and went into the supermarket with me. She was an extension of me and I started to love her like a child.

The day I got her fixed the veterinarian came to my house with his pickup truck. He pulled a small four legged metal table out and a toolbox. She got her shot to fall asleep and was shaved and prepped for the surgery. The doctor splayed her out with ropes on each leg across the metal table on the high ground of the beach. He sanitized and cleaned everything for the surgery and right before he made the incision he made the sign of the cross across his chest. I watched the whole surgery and felt as anxious as I imagine a parent feels watching their child go into surgery.

The school year ended and with it came my time to return home to Michigan. Right before I left I learned that Lycah used to have a previous owner and was born in the middle of October, right around the time I arrived in Samara.

Lycah came home with me on the airplane. As she looked out the window of the airplane in my lap, I told her, "Lycah, you are going to have a wonderful life and you will never be hungry again." We fell asleep together looking out the window. She has never let a day go by without showing how grateful she is and I show her how grateful I am for her getting well and coming home with me. She reminds me every day of the power of love.

"Saving one dog will not change the world, but surely for that one dog, the world will change forever."– Karen Davison

Aaron Hamm *received his bachelor's degree from Central Michigan University in Natural Resources Management in 2012. After college he taught English to grades 1-3 and Environmental Science to grades 9-12 at a small International School in Guanacaste, Costa Rica. He is currently back in school at Ferris State for a B.S degree in Elementary Education. He loves teaching and inspiring young children and sees himself as an elementary science teacher (in a school or an environmental education center) in the not too distant future. In his spare time he enjoys taking Lycah for runs, reading, writing poetry and short stories, and enjoying the wonderful weather of Michigan.*

A Two Way Street

By Sally Karasiewicz

It was a beautiful September day when Roadster was thrown from a moving vehicle and skidded, face first, across the unforgiving pavement. Thanks to good Samaritans, Roadster made his way to Reuben's Room Cat Rescue and Sanctuary, a no-kill shelter in the Grand Rapids area, shortly after his introduction to pavement.

When Roadster came to us he was an extremely thin, dirty orange Maine Coon. He was rushed to a veterinarian who offered little hope for his survival. After the veterinarian provided emergency treatment, he advised Jeanine Buckner (owner/operator of Reuben's Room) to take Roadster home, and if he survived the next 48 hours, to bring him back and they would see what they could do for him. Roadster did survive those 48 hours and began what was to become his odyssey for life and love.

A trip back to the veterinarian provided an extensive work-up. That visit included an x-ray, showing that in-spite of hitting the pavement headfirst, he had not suffered any head injuries. However, his jaw was a severely mangled mess with gaping, open wounds covered in dry, dead skin which had to be cleaned several times over the course of his treatment. Each time this was done, our boy came home with more antibiotics and pain pills.

Due to severe pain, Roadster started out getting his nutrition by patiently licking a can of wet food. Not just any food, our precious guy had to have a specific kind of wet canned food. After several attempts at finding the right canned food, we learned that Roadster would only eat kitten food! Even though Roadster had canned food available at all times, a week later his visit to the veterinarian revealed he had lost 4½ lbs. A week later Roadster was still losing weight. Exploratory surgery and biopsy found the cause of his weight loss—our big boy had cancer.

The cancer cells were removed and when Roadster came home he was like a new cat. He cuddled and played, and of course, like most cats, he catnapped several times a day. He had even gained weight! We were warned his cancer was an aggressive cancer, and it could come back at any time. But he was doing so well, and it looked like he was on the road to recovery, so we tried to put that scary thought aside and believe he had made his last trip to the veterinarian.

Naturally, with everything the rescue went through, Roadster quickly became a "fan favorite" as everyone watched his slow recovery. Our big guy picked out his favorite spot on one of the cat trees where he could keep an eye on everything, and quickly made it known that it was HIS spot. Cats always seem to figure things out quickly and that perch remained open at all times, except of course when Roadster was relaxing or sleeping there. He also staked out his own special sleeping cubby, and again, the other cats had no problem letting him keep that cubby all to himself.

Unfortunately, Roadster started losing weight again. The cancer had returned. Treatment would mean another surgery, and there was no guarantee that the cancer would not once again rear its ugly head. It was determined another surgery would be too rough on Roaster. So he was brought home to Reuben's Room where he could enjoy love and peace for whatever time he had left.

When he came back to the rescue after what was to be his last trip to the veterinarian, Roadster acted just fine, and even started following the volunteers around the rescue like a little puppy dog, just waiting for a volunteer to stop what they were doing and give him some quality one-on-one time.

As time went on, Roadster started sleeping more and eating less. He was still a big cuddler and enjoyed playing, but his play was not as exuberant as it once was. He was spending more time in his cubby and spot on the cat tree. And now he needed to be caged part of each day to make sure he was getting enough nutrition. But Roadster was still our beautiful bright orange Maine Coon who had survived, in-spite of injuries sustained when he was thrown from a moving car. He even made it for a few months in spite of the cancer.

Why was Roadster in such horrible shape when he came to Reuben's Room? Why was he thrown from a moving car? Did his previous family learn about the cancer and decide they did not want to deal with it? Did they subscribe to the belief that animals were disposable? Reuben's Room Cat Rescue and Sanctuary will never know the answers to those questions. What we do know is Roadster had a wonderful life for the few short months he lived at the rescue. Our battered and bruised boy touched the lives of everyone he came in contact with. He wasn't with us for very long, but we were truly blessed he spent his last few months with us. We showered Roadster with love, and he returned that love.

Love is indeed a two way street.

Sally Karasiewicz currently has two cats, a dog, and one 31-year-old cockatiel. In addition, there are four friendly ferals that have taken up residence in her backyard.

As a small child, she dreamed about the possibility of helping animals. Working at Reuben's Room has been a dream come true and she has been a Reuben's Room Cat Rescue and Sanctuary volunteer for 10 years. To learn more about Reuben's Room Cat Rescue and Sanctuary, please check out their website at: *www.reubensroom.petfinder.com.*

Slum Buddy

By Daniel R. Tardona

Often, true treasures of our lives are found in unexpected places. Sometimes fate lends a hand in a chance meeting. In my case, a fortuitous meeting of two inner-city challenged spirits was to become a long and deep friendship. Memories cherished to this day.

Any sensible slum kid knows it is good to be aware of all the slick shortcuts through one's neighborhood. It was crucial knowledge in the squalid and perilous streets of Williamsburg, or Burg, in Brooklyn during the 1960s. Knowing every alleyway, vacant lot, chained link fence-hole and quick cut-through was vital in the daily tasks of getting to school on time, avoiding local street bullies, and getting home before parental curfew. It was during one of my more unhurried forays through one of these urban mazes that led to the meeting of two unlikely companions.

During a foray through a slimy alleyway, I emerged onto a vacant lot. Full of inner-city refuse, patches of urban weeds and ruins of old homes; vacant lots in the Burg were anything but vacant. Explorations of these junk laden lots were always full of adventure, discovery and sometimes the finding of useful treasures. It was amongst the debris of old furniture, window shutters, shards of broken glass, rusted cans, concrete slabs, mangled scrap, and a variety of other waste we called slum slime, that I first set eyes on my future canine buddy. As I alertly crept through the lot, my ears caught movement I thought was a large Norway rat or "slum pig." I soon realized the creature was something larger and potentially more menacing.

The animal was larger than any alley cat, mostly brown and with a tinge of dirty white under his jowls. It was a dog! He noticed me as well—his floppy ears bent flat on his head and he bared his teeth while emitting a long deep growl. The animal looked menacing with a long scar running from the top of his rump and down his left hind leg, and one ear half chewed off. Fear filled my gut. It was one of those moments when all senses become acutely aware. Knowing not to run, I blurted out unintelligible words in the most soothing tone while not moving a muscle. The dog began to relax, which calmed me as well. I kept talking in a gentle and high-toned voice. As we both settled down, I slowly sat right where I stood. I sensed he was not a threat, despite his look of a street worn warrior. In spite of his matted brown coat and less than regal blood line, he stood tall, maintaining an air of dignity and pride. Slowly, while not looking directly in his eyes, I moved in any direction but toward him while constantly and softly jabbering "nice dog" and "do you come here all the time" or "find anything interesting?" Looking back over my shoulder, I noticed he moved with me in a parallel direction to the end of the lot. When I looked toward him, he would look the other way, behaving as if he was not interested. I went on my way through to the next alleyway. He did not follow.

That night in my bed I thought about our meeting and what might happen to him. I wondered if we would meet again. On my next visit to the lot, I anticipated he would not be there, but he appeared behind an old door-less refrigerator lying on its side. Moving around to the side facing me, he laid down, all the time eyeing me. Then he gave a half-hearted bark. His ears were straight up, not back and flattened. His body language suggested he recognized me, but I did not see any happy tail wagging. Staying a good distance away, I perched myself on a discarded milk crate all the while chatting to him softly. Suddenly, he sat with ears up and pointing forward. He seemed to listen to me, never moving in my direction despite my occasional friendly gestures and gentle words to "come boy." After about a half hour, he got up and started foraging the lot for food and water. Rummaging through a paper shopping bag he found something edible, chewing while glancing at me occasionally. Having to move on, I waved, whispering goodbye. He intently watched me, chewing all the time, until we were out of sight of each other.

On my next visit, the dog was in his usual place. I also noticed slum pigs foraging nearby. Perched on a bent and rusted pipe, hidden in the center of a small weed patch was what looked like a common everyday urban pigeon or "slum chicken." Another possible prey source for wandering lot dogs, I thought to myself. I guessed the dog would have attempted to hunt and eat these animals. They all appeared oblivious to each other. I wondered how they all survived. The only viable consistent food source in the poor and densely populated human inner-city streets was the excessive garbage. In hindsight, I realized these animals were well adapted and surviving in their inner-city wilderness much as the bears and elk of a faraway natural wilderness. Before I left this time I decided I would bring the dog nutritious food and perhaps try to get closer to him on the next visit. Maybe then I might try and forge a friendship. As I left, he looked up at me with a curious glance and then went about his business.

When I told my mom about my encounters with the dog and my desire to bring him some food, she responded with doubt and warning. Mom was always loving and supportive of my harebrained adventures and ideas. She also had an un-canny sense of when I was about to get in trouble or be in danger of something. She was afraid this dog could be rabid and forbade me from getting too close. She added I should probably avoid the lot for a few days. While her warnings concerned me a great deal, my own instincts told me she was wrong—at least this time. I would hear nothing of it and decided to spend some of my precious allowance on dog food at Tino's, a grocery store below our flat. To my angst, I also had to buy one of those small metal can openers as there were no "pop top" dog food cans in those days.

On the next visit, following my routine, I sat on the old wooden milk crate, talked a bit and then pulled the food can and opener from my pocket. His ears perked up, even his mangled one which made him look so much less threatening and more friendly than before. Placing the can on the ground a few feet in front of me, I called him over. He crouched down and took a few steps toward the can and me. He approached me little-by-little looking more like a hunting alley cat than a dog. His ears would pop up and down, his tail wagged despite being tucked between his legs. He slunk closer so I could see his scarred nose sniffing away, racking the air for every scent. With drool dripping from his jaws, his head down looking intently at me and then to the can of food, he finally was within inches of me. Reaching the can, he took a quick bite and jerked a few steps back while fixing his eyes on me. He approached again, and devoured the food in seconds. When he finished, he sat looking at me and began to whine. I did not understand, but I took it as a thank you. In hindsight, he was probably still hungry. I returned the next day with another can of food, this time our encounter was more relaxed. Then it happened. He lay on the ground, paws forward almost cradling the can looking up at me. His tail began to wag! When he finished eating, I offered my hand for his inspection. He sniffed at my hand and licked it. His ears were up; his tail was wagging, we were slum buddies from that day on.

Buddy came to live with the family and rarely left my side. He would watch me play stickball and even retrieve the ball when it went under a parked car. Buddy and I were kindred spirits, who loved to explore the world through the rest of my childhood. We rescued each other during difficult times, sharing many adventures. Buddy's spirit remains in my heart, and his memory often helps me even today during difficult times.

Daniel R. Tardona *was born in Brooklyn, New York. His relationship with animals more often came from experiences with the many abandoned dogs and cats roaming inner-city streets just trying to survive, let alone find human companionship. It is his relationships with these animals that provided him opportunities to learn about both he and the animals.*

Daniel has found that each animal companion he rescued has also served to rescue him in at least some small way. His animal friends helped lead him to his life passion of conservation of wildlife and nature, as well as his profession of conservation psychology and National Park Ranger for more than 28 years.

From Death Row to a Forever Home

By Gayle Thompson

The first time I saw Daisy was at the animal shelter. She was sitting in the middle of her kennel trembling—whether she was cold from being nearly hairless or because of fear, I didn't know. Her bald back, which resembled the skin of an elephant in texture and color, revealed fleas running freely over that gray field. The hair she did have on her head, legs, and end of her tail, was sparse and thin. She had a foul odor, and green gobs of goo were matted in the corners of her eyes. She stared at the floor and wouldn't look up at me when I spoke to her.

Having lost my best fur-buddy three weeks previously, I really wasn't in the market for a dog, but my grief was such that I felt the need to be around dogs that day, so I stopped at the shelter. I walked between the cages talking to the dogs and petting them as best I could through the bars, when I came upon Daisy.

While I was looking at Daisy, the shelter director walked down the aisle between the kennels, and I approached her. Pointing to Daisy, I asked, "What's the story with this dog?" She told me that Daisy, a Rottweiler and two cats had been surrendered the day before by a family who had lost their home. Even though the Rottweiler had fleas, he had been adopted the evening before (he had been flea bathed and put on flea preventative before leaving). I asked the director what she thought Daisy's chances were of being adopted, and she told me she wouldn't be putting Daisy up for adoption—she was slated for euthanasia. Daisy was eight years old.

I asked if I could take Daisy for a walk—it just seemed the humane thing to do. The shelter manager agreed and walked with me. Daisy was very good on the leash and did not pull. As we talked, I offered to take Daisy to a vet to see if she could be treated, but was told the shelter didn't have the funds to pay for vet treatment. I said I would pay for treatment, but then was told they didn't have the necessary staff to give Daisy the attention she would need for recuperation. The shelter manager then asked if I would be willing to foster her until she was adoptable. Without thinking, I agreed, and she went inside to make a phone call, while I stood outside with Daisy, asking myself what the heck I was getting into.

The shelter director arranged for me to meet a member of a local rescue group. Daisy was given a flea bath, as well as flea and heartworm preventatives (she had tested negative for heartworm) and brought to my house the following day. We discussed the ins and outs of fostering, I signed an agreement, and we (Daisy and I) were now roommates.

A couple days later, I took Daisy to the vet for a diagnosis and treatment. She was greeted with less than enthusiasm. The vet seemed to think there was little hope of her hair growing back, because of the condition of her skin. She seemed to think the best solution for Daisy would be to put her out of her misery. Daisy also had a bad ear infection. After a phone call to the rescue to voice her own opinion against saving this dog, but being told to give it a month, the vet gave

Daisy some steroids, antibiotics, medicated shampoo, eye ointment, and we left.

The first few days at my house, Daisy was confused and scared and continued to tremble, but she was so appreciative and grateful for any attention I paid to her. I bathed her every third day, and in about ten days, I noticed she seemed to have some sort of white film over her body—I thought I wasn't rinsing her well enough and that residue from the shampoo was lingering on her skin. I wet the tip of my finger and tried to rub off the white residue. When that didn't work, I wet a washcloth and tried to rub it off again, but it wouldn't come off. That's because it was hair—hair just becoming visible.

When I took Daisy back to the vet's office three weeks after her initial appointment, she had hair over her entire body! Now I could see that she was a white dog with big brown areas. The vet tech was so surprised to see her with hair that she kept loudly exclaiming, "Oh, my God, look at that dog! Look at that dog!" She asked if she could take a picture of her and take her in the back to show the rest of the staff.

Over the next four months, Daisy's self-confidence emerged, and she became a playful and well-adjusted dog, running and sprinting and rolling in the grass over my two-and-a-quarter acres. Her hair continued to grow—long and thick and wavy. She was a Welsh springer spaniel! A sweet, gentle dog, I thought she would make a wonderful companion for an elderly couple.

Just before Christmas that year, Daisy found her forever home with a 77-year-old woman. When they met for the first time, it was as if two old friends were reuniting—there was an immediate bond between the two. After a two-hour drive, with Daisy sleeping the whole way, her new mom pulled into her driveway and said, "We're home." She told me that Daisy immediately sat up, as if to say, "Oh, good." She went into the house and made herself right at home, as though she had always lived there. It was a match made in heaven.

Some people say there is no such thing as Divine Intervention, but you could never convince Daisy of that. And as an inspiration to me, I went on to foster other dogs.

Gayle Thompson holds a BA in theater from Naropa University and an almost MA in English Composition and Communication from Central Michigan University. She is a writer of short witty paragraphs—the lot of which have yet to become a book (and who would buy a book of short witty paragraphs, anyway?)—and freelance copy editor. In 1995, about six months after volunteering and then obtaining a part-time position with the animal shelter in Bennington, Vermont, where she was introduced to the up-and-down world of animal rescue, Gayle became actively involved in personally fostering and advocating for companion animals. Since moving back to Michigan, Gayle has continued in that role of fostering and advocating for homeless animals.

You Just Never Know

By Michele J. Dunckel

For a number of years, I was lucky enough to be the proprietor of Cat's Cradle Fine Feline Accommodations, a luxury cat hotel, located in rural southern Michigan adjacent to my home. I designed the building to look like a cottage from the outside, but inside were 30 individual guest rooms, with ancillary space on the second floor. As a result, I had plenty of room to take in kitties that needed to be rescued. Typically, I had 10-12 felines needing a home at any one time and I frequently found these darlings new homes with my clients. I had the assurance they were going to a great home and that I'd probably see them again the next time the client traveled.

One morning a phone call started a chain of events that, even years later, still amazes me.

"Cat's Cradle," I answered brightly.

"I've seen your ads in the paper and I'm hoping you can help me," a desperate-sounding man replied. "I'm at my wit's end with our cat, Snowy. We love him, he's a member of our family, but we just realized he's been peeing in a very specific corner of our carpeted living room. I don't know what to do and our house smells horrible."

My immediate thought was, *If I had a cure for this, I'd knock Oprah out of her spot as richest woman in America.*

Ken, Snowy's owner, explained that Snowy had been urinating on the carpet for quite some time prior to discovery. I advised that removing the odor from the area would be required before trying to change Snowy's behavior. We agreed that Snowy would come stay with me at Cat's Cradle while cleanup was in process, hopeful that confinement would reestablish his hygiene habits.

The whole family brought him in and I had the opportunity to question them about changes in their home that might have triggered Snowy's bad behavior. They seemed to be a happy group, no new pets, no pets had left the home, no new people living in the home, no members had recently left the home, and no changes in food or litter. They had also taken him to their veterinarian and found no physical reason that would account for the change.

I got to know Snowy very well—he was a gentle, affectionate cat, a little on the shy side. At first he was very nervous, but he calmed down and seemed to enjoy his stay. While he was mostly white, he had a few grey patches: one by his right ear, one on this neck and another larger area on the right center of his back. Not once did he urinate anywhere but in his litter box. After a week, Snowy's family took him home, optimistic that he and his litter box were friends again.

Shortly after Snowy's departure, I received a phone call from one of my clients, an elderly gentleman, who was owned by a beautiful cat, Nikki. An apple-head, tortoise-shell seal-point Siamese, she was beloved by Mr. Richards and his wife. Recently though, she was becoming a danger to the aging couple, especially Mrs. Richards who was having trouble getting around. She was in fear of falling when Nikki followed her around and wove herself around her legs. Mr. Richards wondered if I would take her and find her a good home should they decide relinquishing Nikki was the only answer. I assured him I would be happy to take Nikki, while inside I was hoping that wouldn't be necessary. I was concerned about taking in another rescue when I was already at capacity.

Another week went by and Cheryl, Snowy's mom, called. Snowy had been a model cat for the first few days back home, then they noticed that his litter boxes hadn't been used as often as they should have been. They discovered he was up to his old tricks and they returned him to me while they replaced the subfloor of their living room and installed new carpet. They really loved this guy and wanted to do whatever they could to keep him.

He was with me for two weeks while the repairs were being made, and again, he was perfectly behaved. He seemed happy to be back and relaxed the minute he was settled in his room.

Once the repairs were complete, Snowy's parents took him home, and within an hour after they'd left, my phone rang. It was Cheryl. They'd only been home a few minutes when Snowy, in full view of everyone, went back to his favorite corner and peed on the floor. Clearly, Snowy didn't want to be with this family anymore. I agreed to take him and do my best to find him a home where he would be happy. The family brought him back and wept as they said good bye.

For the next few weeks, Snowy was a very happy, loving kitty. He ate well and used his litter box without fail. So it was a shock one morning when I first walked into the hotel to see that something was seriously wrong with him. Being mostly white, his nose, ears, and areas around his eyes were naturally pink. That morning, all those areas were yellow; he wouldn't eat and didn't even move around. I took him to the vet immediately and he was diagnosed as having some sort of an autoimmune issue. They offered little hope and sent me home with medication that might help, but wasn't particularly successful. I was told they rarely saw recovery when the body turns on itself. If the antibiotics worked I would see improvement in 24 hours. If not, there wasn't anything else they could do.

I took Snowy home and kept him as comfortable as I could, and tried my best to get him to eat, offering tuna, chicken and baby food. The next morning he was worse and it became apparent that the kindest thing for Snowy was euthanasia.

With a lump in my throat, I called Snowy's parents and explained the situation. They were again in tears as they agreed there was only one, loving option. I took Snowy back to the veterinarian's office and held his paw for his last few moments of life.

Exactly one week after Snowy passed, Mr. Richard's daughter called me. A very pleasant woman, we had a very friendly chat, mostly about Nikki.

"So, my father told me he'd spoken with you and you agreed to take Nikki," she eventually said. "I just wanted to make sure."

"Yes, I will certainly take her. I expect I'll be able to find her a great home," I replied. "When did your parents want to bring her out?"

"Oh," She inhaled sharply, "I guess you don't know. My father died."

A beat of silence from me.

"I'm so sorry," I said when I recovered from the unexpected news. "When did he pass?"

"Last Tuesday," she responded.

It was the same day we put Snowy down. Without a doubt, Nikki was meant to be with me.

Nikki lived at Cat's Cradle for about a year. Several people wanted to adopt her, but she gave them a cold shoulder and a couple of hisses, until the day she decided she wanted my office manager, Judy, to adopt her. Nikki was loved and happy with Judy until Nikki died many years later.

Epilogue

Shortly after Nikki came to live with me, a local breeder of Siamese cats, Shirley, brought her breeding stock to stay with me while she had work done in her home. She recognized Nikki immediately as one of her kittens. She was very sad the Richards had had to give her up, but very happy she'd come to a safe place.

Two years later, on a very hot, muggy afternoon, the breeder once again brought her cats to me, and this time it included a litter of six-week old kittens. I was very excited to see them. At the time I and my relatives were keeping vigil at the side of my dying husband. He seemed to be resting comfortably, so when I saw Shirley had arrived, I ran out briefly to say hello. While I was doing so, my husband passed away. Shirley felt horrible, though she of course had no reason, but she came to the church during the funeral and helped with all the things that needed to be done. We remained close until I moved to Boston.

In reading this story and the others in this book, you'll see that when you rescue an animal, you just never know where the path will lead and goodness will come back to you many times over.

*A passionate animal lover, **Michele J. Dunckel** has been caring for and rescuing cats for over 60 years. She created a luxury cat hotel which also accommodated cats and kittens* *rescued by clients, the humane society and Michele herself. Michele has since retired and moved to Boston, where she continues rescue work providing foster care services. She currently has six cats of her own, all rescues. She's been writing almost as long as she has cared for cats and writes a bi-monthly cat column for a Michigan pet publication.*

Turtle Rescue

By Sue Merrell

Gwen Black noticed the turtle first. A green sea turtle—about the size and shape of a large Chicago-style deep-dish pizza—was swimming about 50 feet from her dock on Little Torch Key.

Gwen and her husband Larry are Canadians who like to spend a few months each winter renting a house in the Florida Keys. Their spot is ideal on the open water. We were about to go kayaking when Gwen spotted the turtle. At first she couldn't believe her luck. The turtle was swimming back and forth in a small area, close enough to be photographed from the shore.

Larry was using the zoom feature on his smart phone camera when he spotted a growth on the turtle's face. Each of us examined the photo on the phone. There did indeed appear to be a white tumor of some sort near the turtle's eye.

I had recently toured the Turtle Hospital in Marathon, about 20 miles east of Little Torch. I knew that when a turtle's shell is cracked by a boat propeller or animal strike, an air pocket can form inside the shell making it hard for the turtle to swim to the bottom to eat. Was that why this turtle was staying on the top so long?

Gwen became concerned and called the turtle hospital.

Begun in 1993 in a remodeled bar, Marathon's Turtle Hospital is the only state-certified veterinary hospital in the world for sea turtles. More than half of the hospital's equipment has been donated by doctors, hospitals and individuals. The veterinarians of Marathon Animal Hospital donate their time. The facility, which is open for tours, includes a sparkling operating room and high tech x-ray equipment. Behind the facility are 23 individual pools to house the turtles as they regain their strength. There's also a full-size swimming pool for turtles. Many take a year or more to recover before they are released back into the ocean.

In the past year, the hospital had admitted 60 turtles. Of that number, 39 were Greens, 17 were Loggerheads, three were Hawksbills (all post hatchlings), and one was a Kemp's Ridley. Also that year, the hospital was able to return 24 patients back to good health and release them back into the ocean.

The hospital also received more than 100 loggerhead hatchlings that were found by volunteers. These baby turtles were either unable to crawl out of the nest, had crawled into the mangroves instead of the sea, or had been picked up by birds and dropped into storm drains. The hospital was able to release about 75 percent of these foundlings into the Gulf Stream, 20-30 miles offshore where they had a decent chance to live a long and healthy life.

When Gwen called the hospital and reported the turtle's sickly behavior, a turtle ambulance was dispatched immediately. Rehab specialist Devin arrived in about 20 minutes. She put on a snorkel, strapped a video camera to her head and swam out to where the turtle was still floating. She hovered over him a few seconds and then dove down about two feet and grabbed the turtle by his front flippers. The turtle didn't put up much of a fight. Devin swam to shore and put the turtle into a plastic tub. She immediately took his temperature and pulse. He was very sick.

Right away we noticed the turtle had lots of white cauliflower-like growths all over his body. These were called fibro papillomatosis, a disease reaching epidemic proportions among sea turtles. It was caused by a herpes-like virus. Because the growths looked like barnacles, we quickly named the turtle Barney.

Upon arrival at the Turtle Hospital, the staff discovered that Barney had either suffered a boat propeller strike or a large predator attack. A large and small crack consumed the whole left side of the turtle's carapace and a small puncture wound was also noted on the underside. Turtle Hospital staff members were afraid Barney might not make it through the night due to his low blood levels, but he pulled through.

The following morning the algae was wiped free from his shell and he was put out back in a shallow water tank. Barney seemed alert and improving.

Barney arrived at the hospital in March. Over the next few months, he received several surgeries to remove external tumors. But in June, the staff discovered internal tumors. About 20 percent of turtles with fibro papillomatosis develop internal tumors in their lungs and other organs. Barney had to be euthanized.

Not every turtle can be saved, but the Marathon Turtle Hospital continues its work to save as many as it can. Just before Christmas, the hospital received word that 40 Kemps Ridley turtles that normally migrate south had become stuck off Cape Cod, Massachusetts. The young turtles were rescued and flown to Florida to be distributed among various marine facilities, including the Turtle Hospital, for rehabilitation and release.

So what can you do?

- **Contribute** to conservation organizations and rehabilitation centers. Checks may be sent to
The Turtle Hospital
2396 Overseas Highway
Marathon Florida 33050.

- **Reduce, Reuse, Recycle.** Buy products with less packaging (especially fresh produce). Reuse what you can and recycle what you cannot. Get a reusable water bottle instead of using endless plastic water bottles. A plastic water bottle is used for five minutes and is around for 500 years. A recent study found that on average our oceans are littered with 47,000 pieces of plastic per square mile!

- **If you see an animal in distress, call for help.**

Sue Merrell worked more than 30 years for newspapers in Texas, South Carolina, Illinois and Michigan, covering everything from the cops beat to writing a singles column and editing a food section. She spent the last 10 years of her fulltime journalism career reviewing theater for The Grand Rapids Press. Soon after retiring in 2009, she wrote a memoir, Laughing for a Living. In 2010, she launched a mystery/thriller series with Great News Town, followed by One Shoe Off, in 2012 and Full Moon Friday in 2014. She spends her summers on a lake in Grandville, MI, and winters in the Florida Keys.

About the Editors

Tricia L. McDonald is owner and operator of Splattered Ink Press (www.splatteredinkpress.com). A writing coach, author, and public speaker, Tricia also teaches writing classes and volunteers at several senior citizens' facilities where she facilitates writing groups.

As an internationally published author, Tricia's Life With Sally series (*Little White Dog Tails, Still Spinnin' Tails, and Waggin' More Tails*) chronicles life with her miniature bull terrier. She also writes a monthly column, Life with Sally, for *Cats and Dogs Magazine*. Tricia's book *Quit Whining Start Writing* is a guide for writers to assist them in putting away their excuses and accomplishing their writing goals.

Janet Vormittag is the author of two novels, *Dog 281* and its sequel, *More Than a Number*. She is the founder and publisher of *Cats and Dogs, a Magazine Devoted to Companion Animals*. The free publication, distributed in West Michigan, celebrates human-animal relationships and promotes pet adoption and spay/neuter.

Janet has a bachelor's degree in journalism from Grand Valley State University and was a freelance correspondent for The Grand Rapids Press for ten years. She is a member of GVSU Allendale Toastmasters. www.janetvormittag.com